cook at home with peter gordon

also by peter gordon
the sugar club cookbook

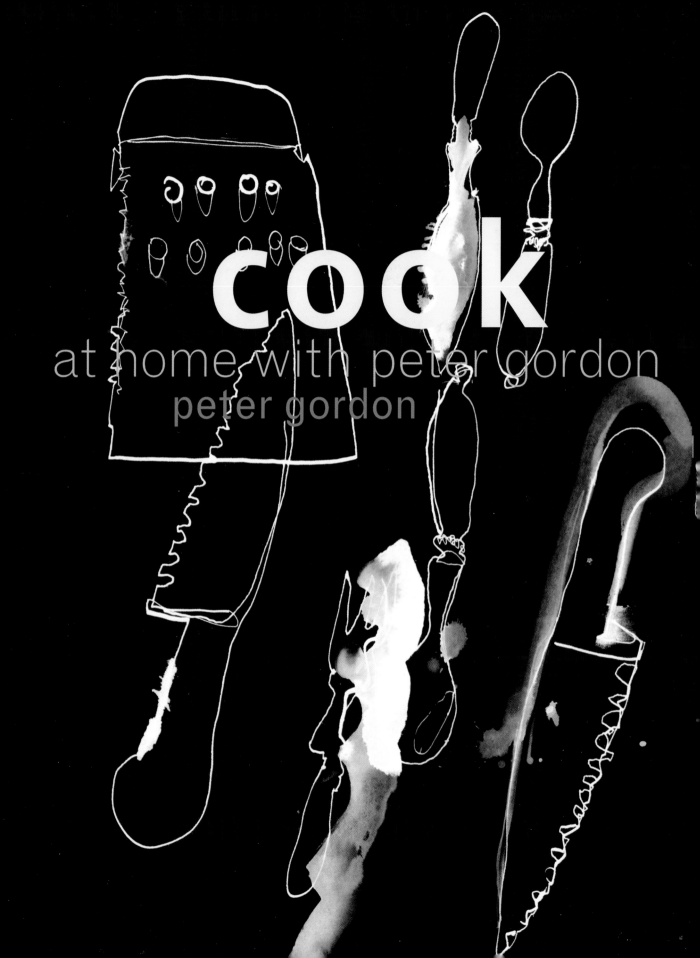

cook

at home with peter gordon
peter gordon

acknowledgments

This book is dedicated to my family, and especially to my partner Michael McGrath. Those of you who bought my first book have encouraged Martin Neild and Sue Fletcher at Hodder & Stoughton to commission me to write this, so I thank you. Felicity Rubinstein, my agent, gets special thanks for holding me together. I hope you'll like this book as much as I do, which is also thanks to the work of Jean Cazals, Moira Bogue and Trevor Flynn, who've made it all look so beautiful.

Peter Gordon would be happy to hear from readers with their comments on the book at the following e-mail address: peter@foodware.demon.co.uk

oven temperature conversion table

110°c	*=*	*225°f*
140°c	*=*	*280°f*
160°c	*=*	*325°f*
180°c	*=*	*350°f*
190°c	*=*	*375°f*
200°c	*=*	*390°f*
210°c	*=*	*430°f*

every oven varies slightly and you will know your oven best,
but in most recipes the precise temperature is not crucial.

Design by Moira Bogue
Photographs & Styling by Jean Cazals
Illustrations by Trevor Flynn

Copyright © 1999 Peter Gordon

The right of Peter Gordon to be identified as the Author of the Work has been asserted by him in accordance with the Copyright, Designs and Patents Act 1988.

First published in Great Britain in 1999 by Hodder & Stoughton
A division of Hodder Headline PLC

10 9 8 7 6 5 4 3 2 1

A CIP catalogue record for this title is available from the British Library

ISBN 0 340 71856 0

Printed and bound by The Bath Press

Hodder & Stoughton
A division of Hodder Headline PLC
338 Euston Road
London NW1 3BH

contents

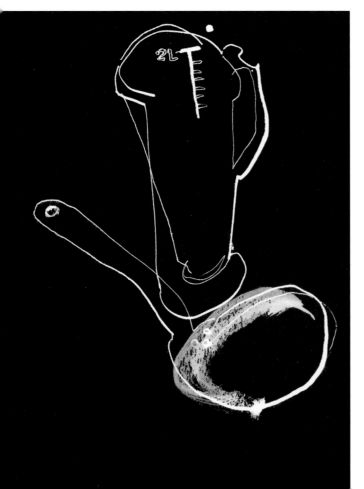

introduction

Some of you, flicking through these pages and reading my recipes for the first time, might be thinking that some of the ingredients I use are pretty wild and wacky. Some of them may even be a total mystery to you. Don't worry! They are also readily available and simple to use. This new book is dedicated to anyone who wants to use the flavours that I love so much myself, but in a more homely way … maybe adding a dash of Thai fish sauce to stewed tomatoes for breakfast, for example, or throwing a bit of coriander into a crab omelette for a quiet dinner party, or even simmering garlic and ginger with lemon and honey to combat a dose of flu.

I know from correspondence with those of you who bought my first book, *The Sugar Club Cookbook*, that you bought lots of new ingredients and are thinking 'What do I do with all the left overs?'. Luckily, a host of supermarkets are now selling many of those ingredients: tamarind paste and smoked paprika (two favourites) are now common-place country-wide. I've also had a great deal of positive feedback from people I've encouraged to source their supplies from ethnic food-shops all over the country. Many people had never ventured into these stores because they seemed so alien; now they appear more like a welcoming treasure trove. So, when you're out buying ingredients for recipes from this book, it will be that much easier.

Many things have changed since I wrote *The Sugar Club Cookbook*, the most obvious being the Sugar Club's relocation to London's West Soho – not an easy move, and a much more demanding set-up than the one in Notting Hill. The new restaurant is more than twice the size; the numbers of staff have doubled … and I have a sneaking suspicion that I've had about half as much sleep since we first opened the place in July 1998! My kitchen team is much larger, obviously, and we have an extra oven and deep-fryer, and a walk-in cool-room. What was formerly the Sugar Club in Notting Hill has become the Bali Sugar, with Ashley Sumner and Vivienne Hayman still its owners.

A highlight of this year was being named New Zealander of the Year at the Savoy by the New Zealand Society. As well as writing for three different monthly magazines, I was also lucky enough to be on six episodes of Nigel Slater's television series on Channel 4 – which I enjoyed enormously – making sandwiches, ice cream and other dishes. Earlier this year, Sophie Grigson came to watch me cook a very smoky halibut in curry leaves with mango sauce, for her 'Herb' series on the BBC, and came shopping with me at my favourite food shop, Foodworld, on the Kilburn High Road – an emporium full of delicious treats from all over Asia and the Middle East.

Recently my partner Michael and I managed to get to Spain and Italy again, for a couple of short breaks. I do love Spain, and for this, our third visit, we went to Andalucia – an extraordinarily beautiful region with equally delicious food. The flavours are incredibly robust and are complemented perfectly by the local creamy

manzanillas and sherries. (I fell in love with sherry for the first time in Andalucia, as my only other experience of it was years ago, when I secretly had a glug from a bottle in my Grandmother's liquor-cabinet; I now know it was well past its best.)

Sitting in Seville and Cadiz, eating jamòn Jabugo or deepfried prawns, washed down with a cold glass of fino, we felt extremely content. Later, we stayed with old friends Stephen Smith and Marina Perotti in Florence. These days Stephen and Marina are practically vegetarians, except for the odd piece of fish, so on this visit we ate white truffles with potato gnocchi, doused with the new season's olive oil which we'd bought from the Selvapiana vineyard. Federico, who made the olive oil and who is also a wine producer of note, escorted us on a walk around his vineyard: an amazing sight as the early snow wafted around us in the intense winter sunlight. We'd bought the truffles at a truffle festival in San Miniato, a village just outside Pisa. It seemed as if the entire town had crowded into the ancient fresco-painted town hall to gobble up these fabulous oddities. Looking around us at everyone laughing, talking and feasting, people from all walks of life united in their enjoyment, I was thrilled once more to realise the importance of food not just to sustain and refresh with its endless possibilities – but also as an indulgent social pleasure.

I hope you enjoy making the following dishes as much as I have creating and cooking them myself. Please let me know what you think, either by e-mail (peter@foodware.demon.co.uk) or by letter to the publishers. I hope you will also enjoy allowing some of the flavours I savour into your favourite recipes and dishes. Remember that a recipe is there to be adapted by the person cooking it, as they see fit. Use the best produce you can afford (I always use free-range eggs and organic meat and poultry, but have not spelt this out in every recipe); get your supermarket to source ingredients for you that are hard to find (they rely on feedback too) and don't be scared to experiment a little. Most important of all, feel as relaxed as possible when you start cooking; ask your friends to help out a little, and then sit down and relish what you've created ... or else what is the point?

Delight in cooking at home for those that you love.

BREAKFAST

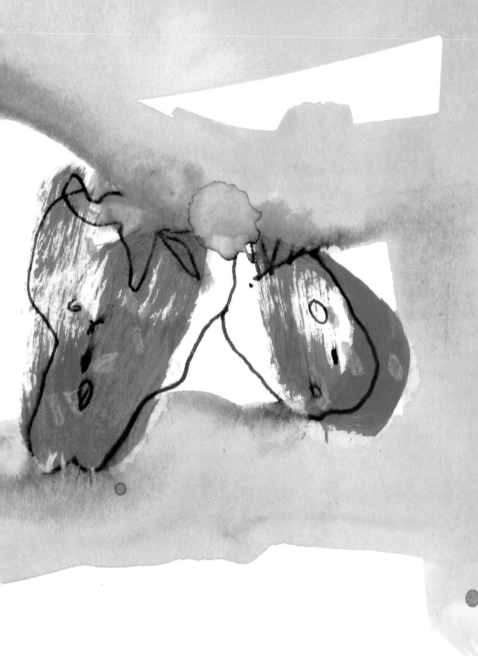

I really enjoy a good breakfast,

...but rarely have time for more than a quick coffee and a slice of toast. On days when I do have time, though, I like to make breakfast into a real production number where anything goes. In Asia, I have even eaten things like coconut curry and fried noodles for breakfast! When as a child I was in New Zealand, and my mad dad Bruce was a keen sea-fisherman, we often had fish we'd caught that morning, as the sun was coming up, fried in butter, before heading off to school.

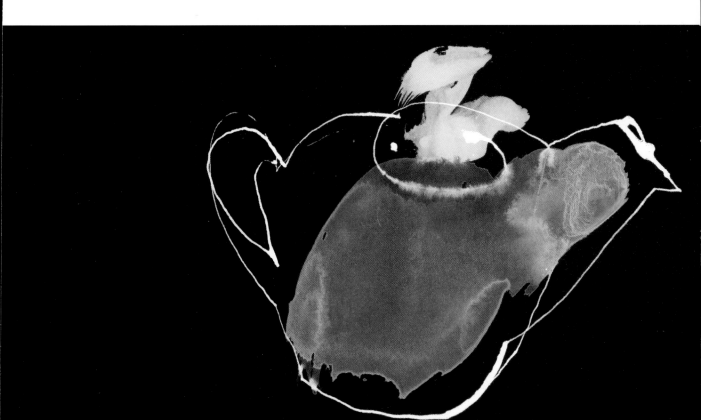

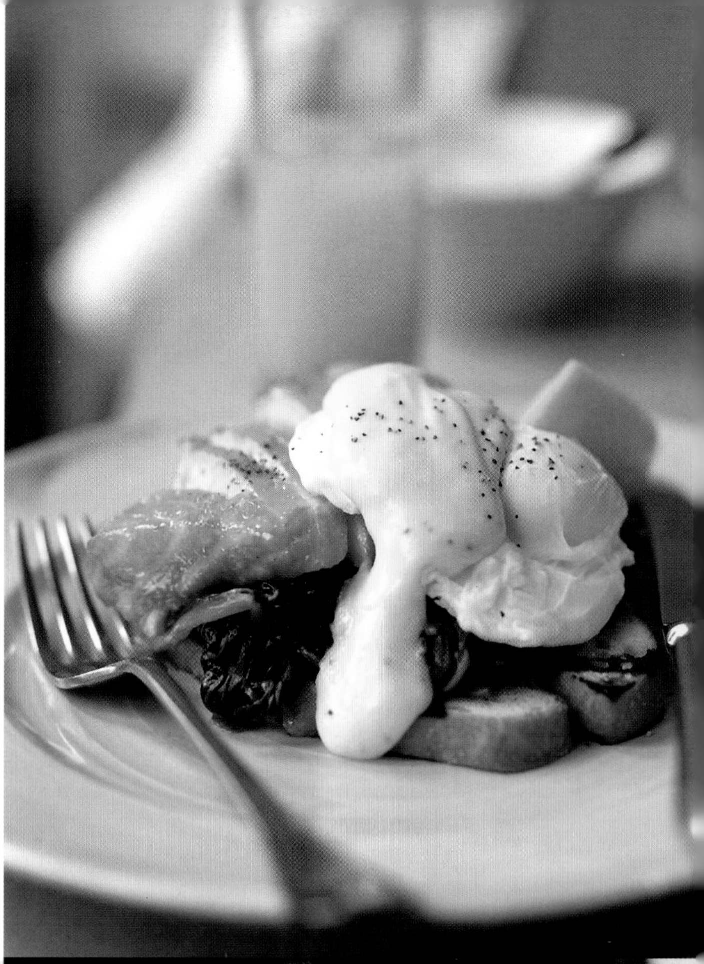

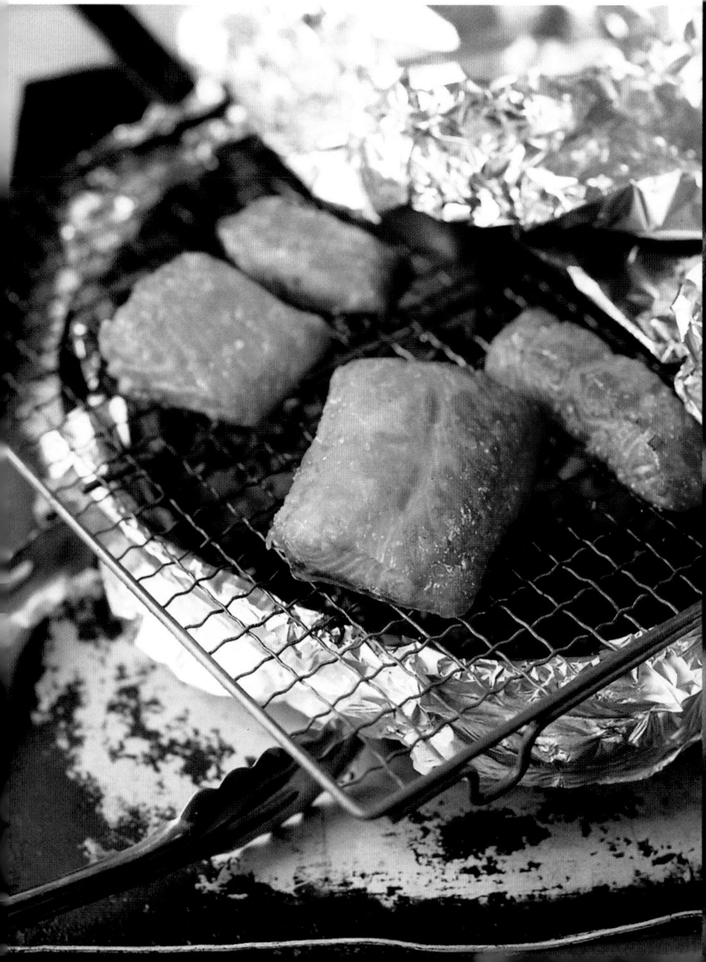

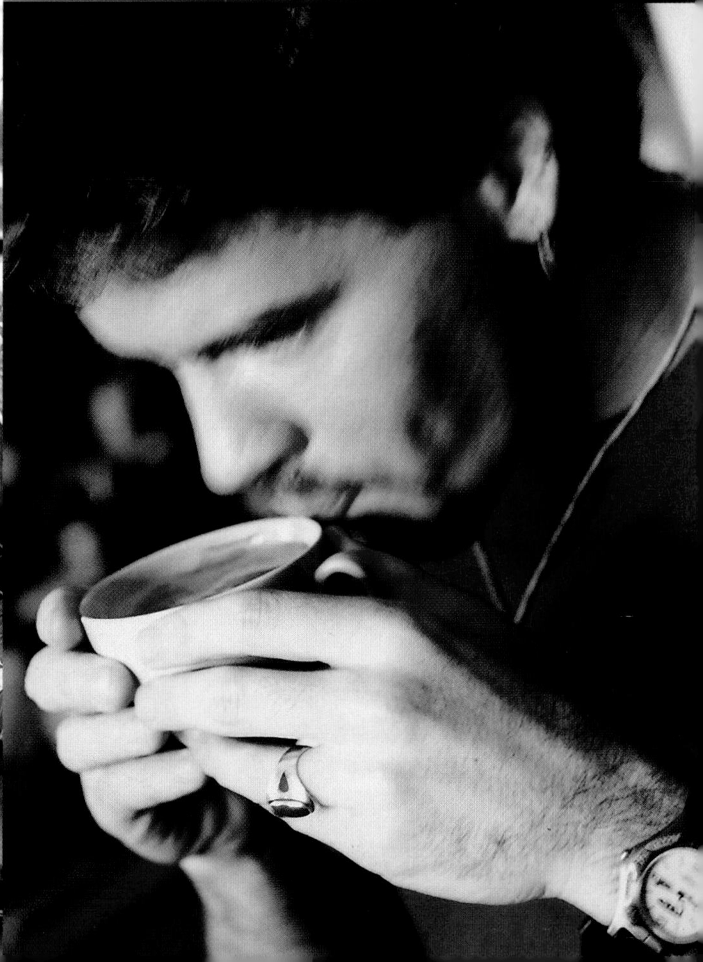

tea-smoked salmon
with poached eggs, toast, spinach and hollandaise

I have to admit I wouldn't want to get up every morning and do tea-smoking before breakfast! But this is a great weekend brekky or brunch dish. This recipe may be the longest and seemingly most complicated in the book, but don't be alarmed: the method tells you how to poach eggs, sauté spinach and make hollandaise. The tea-smoking will create a lot of smoke and a smell to match, so it's best done outside – although I *have* made it with a strong extractor fan, open windows and the promise of a memorable breakfast! Although you only need 500 g of salmon for this dish, I recommend that you smoke at least 1 kg at a time as the effort involved is not light. You can do this up to 4 days ahead, then cool the salmon and store it in the fridge. Any left overs make great sandwiches, with cucumber and mayonnaise. Alternatively, buy some good, hot-smoked salmon such as I found in the village of Orford where they also smoke stilton, mallard and pork knuckles glazed with treacle – but that's another recipe! *For photographs see page 14*

FOR 4

salmon fillet	*1 kg, skin and pin-bones removed*
demerara sugar	*150 g*
sea salt	*200 g, I use maldon*
light olive oil	*30 ml*
white rice	*120 g, uncooked*
tea leaves	*100 g, strong black*
butter	*300 g*
eggs	*10*
egg yolk	*1*
lemon juice	*30 ml*
vinegar	*10 ml, for poaching the eggs*
spinach	*300 g, washed and drained*

Cut the salmon into 2 pieces then lay it in a dish and sprinkle on the sugar, salt and oil. Rub it in well, then turn over the fish and repeat on the other side. Leave to sit at room temperature for 45 minutes, then wipe any excess salt and sugar off the fish.

Ideally, for smoking fish, you need a heavy-bottomed metal roasting tin with a tight-fitting lid, preferably just a little bigger than the salmon fillet, a cake rack to hold the fish 4-6cm above the tea leaves, and 4 metal ramekins, on which to sit the rack. Or if you have a wok with a lid and a circular rack that fits inside it, you're on course. However, as you'll see in the photo, I used a frying-pan, a cake rack that was too big with foil for the lid – so you can smoke your salmon with makeshift alternatives! Line the tin/wok/frying-pan with foil then pour in the rice and tea and mix well. Sit the rack on the ramekins in the dish. When the salmon has marinated, place the tin over a high heat with the lid on. Leave it until smoke starts to billow from it. Then take the lid off – don't put your head over it or you'll choke – and lay the fish quickly on the rack, then replace the lid. Leave over the heat for 2 minutes, then turn it down to medium and continue smoking for another 4 minutes. If you are smoking outside, and can't reduce the heat, decrease smoking time by 1 minute. (The best salmon is always a little raw in the middle, but don't worry if you overcook it as it will still taste great if a little dry.) Turn off the heat and leave for 10 minutes. Remove the lid and sit the salmon, still on its rack, on a tray. (I pour some cold water on the smoking tea to make sure all the heat has subsided before discarding it, wrapped in the foil.)

To make the hollandaise, place 250g of the butter in a small pan and let it melt over a moderate heat. It will separate into a clear yellow fat with a milky white liquid. Keep it warm on the side of the stove. Take a saucepan about 24cm in diameter, and fill it with 6cm of water, bring it to the boil then reduce to a rapid simmer. Take a metal bowl, about 30cm in diameter, that will sit on top of the saucepan, and put in 2 eggs, plus the yolk with the lemon juice. Whisk well, then place the bowl over the simmering water and beat until the mixture thickens. Take the pan off the heat and whisk in the melted butter slowly in 6 reasonably equal amounts – you'll have to guess this. Some people discard the white milky liquid, but I recommend that you add it. It is a little salty and I whisk it in to thin the sauce and also to season it. When the hollandaise is ready, leave it in a warm place until you're ready to serve.

Now poach the remaining eggs. Everyone has their favourite way of doing this, but I add the vinegar to a frying-pan filled with 5cm simmering water, swirl it around, then quickly crack in the eggs. Bring the water back to a simmer, turn down the heat to low and poach for 3-5 minutes depending on how firm you want the yolks. I like mine runny. Meanwhile, sauté the spinach in the remaining 50g of butter, and season it with salt and pepper. Toast the bread.

To serve, place the spinach, salmon and eggs on the toast, spoon over the hollandaise and grind on some black pepper. Then enjoy the rich, buttery, smoky, creamy, crunchy creation you've worked so hard at making (and tell me it was worth the effort!).

bruce gordon's
tomato and bacon soufflé omelette

My father used to love cooking breakfast for the family on Sunday mornings. In fact, he still does. This recipe was his favourite fry-up. Directly he started cooking, we kids would cycle down to the Buy Well supermarket in Putiki Street, and purchase these incredibly doughy white loaves, still warm from the oven. They were known locally, and rather obscurely, as 'barracudas'. Then we'd toast big, thick slabs of the bread and butter them mercilessly. Dad finally served the omelette, hot and sizzling from the pan, on top of these delicious doorsteps. To make this exactly the way Dad did, you'll need a deep frying-pan with a lid.

FOR 4

smoked bacon	*8 rashers, cut into finger-sized pieces*
salted butter	*150 g*
large onion	*1, peeled and finely sliced*
garden fresh tomatoes	*4, quartered*
eggs	*6, separated*
salt	
black pepper	*freshly ground*
hard cheese	*120 g grated, something like cheddar*

Turn the grill on full. Heat the frying-pan on the stove and put in the bacon and 50g of the butter. Fry for a minute, then add the onion and cook until it begins to caramelise a little. Add the tomatoes and cook on a moderate heat for 2-3 minutes, stirring so that they don't stick to the pan.

In a bowl whisk the egg yolks with a fork, then stir in the bacon mixture with a teaspoon of pepper. In another bowl, beat the egg whites to form stiff peaks, adding 1/2 teaspoon salt as you go, then fold them into the bacon mixture. Don't worry if there are lumps of egg white – Dad never did.

Return the frying-pan to the heat, and when it begins to smoke add the rest of the butter. When it has all melted pour in the omelette mixture, and turn down the heat to moderate. Put a lid on the pan and cook for 1 minute, then check to make sure it isn't burning on the bottom – turn the heat down if it is. Sprinkle the cheese on top, put the lid back on and cook for a further minute. Now place the pan under the grill and leave it until the cheese melts. Serve at once on buttered white toast.

stewed tomatoes with coriander, chilli and basil

These are great on toast, either alone, or with sausages, bacon or fried eggs. Apparently they're a bit of a hangover cure!

For photograph see page 15

FOR 4

butter	*100 g*
medium red onions	*2, peeled and finely sliced*
red chilli	*1, finely sliced*
tomatoes	*6, ripe medium-sized, quartered*
thai fish sauce	*1 teaspoon*
coriander leaves	*a big handful*
basil leaves	*a big handful*
black pepper	*freshly ground*

Heat a saucepan and put in the butter. When it has melted, but before it starts to brown, add the onion and chilli and turn the heat up high. Fry for 2 minutes, stirring every now and then, then add the tomatoes and fish sauce and stir well. Fry for a minute or two, until some of the juice runs from the tomatoes, then stir in the herbs. Take off the heat and sprinkle over some freshly ground pepper. Eat on toast.

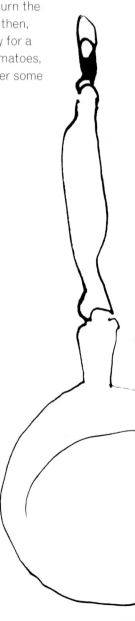

sausage slices in batter

During school holidays my siblings and I loved to make this for breakfast. We used left-over sausages or sometimes shredded slices of luncheon meat. We liked the fritters served on toast, drowned in tomato ketchup.

FOR 2

eggs	*2*
self-raising flour	*50 g*
salt	*1/4 teaspoon*
milk	*200 ml*
sausages	*3, cooked, cut in half lengthways*
butter or	*oil for cooking*

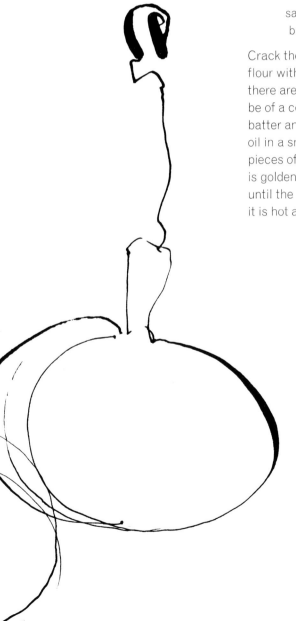

Crack the eggs into a bowl and whisk them together. Sift the flour with the salt, tip it into the eggs and whisk again, until there are no lumps, then beat in the milk. The batter should be of a coating consistency. Drop the sausage slices into the batter and mix well to coat them evenly. Heat a little butter or oil in a small frying-pan, and when it begins to smoke, add 3 pieces of sausage and half of the batter. Cook until the bottom is golden, then flip over the fritter and cook on the other side until the batter is set. Remove it from the pan and eat it while it is hot as you make the next one.

ubud's black rice pudding
with bananas, palm sugar and coconut milk

Ubud is a fairly quiet town, by Balinese standards, located towards the centre of the island. It's an idyllic artistic retreat, set among the rice-paddies. The first time I went there in 1985, I found a thriving night-time food market, where I ate satay, rice cakes, suckling pig and all manner of delicious things. By my third visit in 1989, the market had been closed down: it was not considered suitable for tourists – that's modern thinking for you. However, I discovered this delicious breakfast dish. At first it seems a little bizarre – cold sweet black rice and banana pudding? – but, trust me, it's fantastic. Serve it hot in winter, either for breakfast or dessert, but in summer try it cold, straight from the fridge. You'll find black rice and palm sugar in Indonesian, Thai and larger Chinese food stores. Don't confuse black rice with Canadian wild rice: they are two different grains. The salt mixed in with the coconut milk seems odd too, but it's magic. This will keep for just a day in the fridge.

FOR 6 BREAKFAST PORTIONS

black rice	*400 g, or arborio rice*
water	*900 ml*
ripe bananas	*3*
demerara sugar	*150 g*
salt	*a small pinch*
unsweetened coconut milk	*40 ml*
palm sugar	*150 g, or demerara*

Rinse the rice thoroughly in lots of cold water, then drain it through a sieve. Put it into a saucepan with the water and place, uncovered, on the stove. Bring to the boil, stirring occasionally, then turn down the heat very low, place a lid on the pot, and simmer for 30-35 minutes. The rice should be just *al dente* – give it a few more minutes if necessary.

Peel and cut the bananas into 1/2cm slices and add to the rice together with the demerara sugar. Stir well, and continue to simmer with the lid on for 4 minutes. Stir again – avoid mashing up the bananas – then take the pan off the heat and leave it to cool with the lid on (unless you want to eat the rice pudding hot). The rice should look a little mushy and moist; if it seems dry, add a little boiling water.

Dissolve the salt in the coconut milk. Grate the palm sugar coarsely on a cheese grater. (If it is too soft to grate, warm it gently in a small pan to melt it.)

To serve, spoon the rice mixture – either hot or cold – into individual dishes, pour on some of the coconut milk, then either sprinkle or drizzle over the palm sugar.

michael's toasted oat porridge
with soya milk and maple syrup

Michael McGrath, my partner, makes the best porridge in the world. It's the light toasting of the oats – an idea he picked up when he cooked macrobiotically – that gives it such a delicious taste. He always makes it with a type of soya milk sweetened with apple juice, but regular milk and a little sugar will be fine. At a pinch you could also substitute golden syrup for maple syrup.

FOR 2

organic porridge oats	*140 g*
cold water	*250 ml*
salt	*2 generous pinches*
organic soya milk	*250 ml, sweetened with apple juice (see above)*
maple syrup	*50 ml*

Place the oats in a saucepan and cook them, stirring continuously to prevent burning, over a moderate to high heat for about 2 minutes to toast them lightly. You can tell when they're ready as they'll give off a lovely smell, but won't have coloured much. Take the saucepan to the sink and run cold water over the outside of it to cool it down – this will prevent lumps forming. Add the water and salt, place the saucepan on a moderate heat and stir continuously, until it just comes to the boil. Add the soya milk, and cook gently for a minimum of 5 minutes – longer if you have time as this makes the porridge even creamier – stirring frequently. It should eventually begin to 'bubble and plop, resembling the Rotorua mud pools in New Zealand', according to Michael. Stir in the maple syrup and pour into 2 bowls. Pour on more soya milk, straight from the fridge, and extra maple syrup to taste.

You can add some sliced bananas, apples or sultanas to boost the flavour – I prefer it kept simple – just so long as you use the best organic oats, organic soya milk and maple syrup.

sweetcorn fritters with bacon and maple syrup

This dish has a particularly Antipodean feel to it. You'll encounter it in numerous cafés all over Australia and New Zealand – or variations of it anyway. I like smoked streaky bacon at breakfast, but you could also serve grilled chorizo with this.

FOR 4

sweetcorn	*400 g tinned, drained*
large eggs	*3*
sour cream	*150 ml, or double cream*
polenta	*60 g*
cornflour	*30 g*
spring onions	*1/4 cup, finely sliced*
salt	*1/2 teaspoon*
black pepper	*1/2 teaspoon, freshly ground*
oil	*for frying*
bacon	*400 g smoked, streaky, grilled until crisp*
maple syrup	*100 ml*

Mix together the first 8 ingredients in a large bowl. Heat a frying-pan and add a little oil. Spoon into the hot pan a quarter of the fritter mixture, and cook it for 1-2 minutes until it is golden underneath. Using a wide spatula, flip it over carefully and cook it on the other side for a minute, then remove to a warm plate while you cook the rest. Repeat 3 times with the remaining mixture. Serve the fritters with the bacon on top and the syrup drizzled over.

mango, lime and strawberry salad
with greek yoghurt, toasted oats and honey

A bowl of fresh fruit is a great way to start the day and toasted oats add a lovely crunch. Mangoes and strawberries go together really well, and the lime juice brings out their flavours, but you can make this with your favourite fruit, and substitute grapefruit or orange juice if limes aren't available.

FOR 2

oats	*50 g*
large ripe mango	*1, a little soft to the touch*
fresh lime juice	*30 ml*
strawberries	*8, large, hulled and halved*
greek-style yoghurt	*150 ml*
runny honey	*50 ml*

Lightly toast the oats in a frying-pan over a moderate heat, stirring well to prevent them burning. Once they have taken on a light golden colour, tip them on to a plate and leave them to cool. (You could do a large batch of oats in the oven, as they will keep well in an airtight container for a few weeks.) Meanwhile, peel the mango with either a potato peeler or small knife and then slice the flesh off either side of the stone with a sharp knife. Scrape off any other pieces that cling to the stone. Cut the mango into 1-2 cm pieces and put into a bowl, sprinkle over the lime juice, add the strawberries and stir. Divide the fruit between 2 bowls, dollop some yoghurt over it, then the oats. Lastly pour over the honey.

banana and coconut pancakes,
'traveller style', with honey

You can eat these pancakes either as a breakfast treat or as a dessert, finished with a scoop of good vanilla ice cream. I first had them in Bali, where they seem to appear on most café menus. In the village of Mustang, in Nepal, I ate them made with locally grown apples instead of bananas. They are especially good with bacon or chorizo on top, and drizzled with a little maple syrup. Make them in a 12-15 cm non-stick frying-pan. This will make 4 pancakes, enough for 4 people as a breakfast dish.

FOR 4

large eggs	*2*
palm sugar	*20 g, or golden caster sugar*
plain flour	*150 g*
baking powder	*2 level teaspoons*
salt	*1/4 teaspoon*
unsweetened coconut milk	*250 ml*
cooking oil	*4 teaspoons*
bananas	*2, peeled and sliced into 1cm-thick slices*
long-shredded coconut	*80 g (desiccated coconut will do)*
honey	*100 ml, melted slightly*

Put the eggs and the sugar into a food-processor and blitz for 15 seconds. Add the flour, baking powder and salt and blitz again, then scrape down the sides of the bowl with a spatula. With the motor running, add the coconut milk in a steady stream to make a thickish but pourable batter. Heat a frying-pan, then put in 1 teaspoon of the cooking oil. Pour in a quarter of the batter, scatter on a quarter of the banana pieces and a quarter of the coconut, then gently press them into the batter. Cook over a moderate heat until the pancake looks set, then flip it over carefully and cook for 1 minute to caramelise the banana slightly. Tip the pancake on to a warm plate and repeat 3 times with the remaining oil and mixture. Keep them warm in an oven at a low temperature, or serve as soon as they're made, like we do at home as they're best eaten straight away. Drizzle with the honey.

banana, palm sugar and apple smoothie

A smoothie can be the perfect answer for an on-the-run but satisfying breakfast. I make them with organic soya milk but regular milk works just as well.

FOR 2

bananas	*2, ripe, peeled and halved*
yoghurt	*300 ml*
palm sugar	*2 tablespoons, grated, or demerara sugar*
apples	*2, peeled, cored and quartered*
organic soya milk	*400 ml*

Put all of the above in a blender and purée for 1 minute. Drink.

LUNCH AND SUPPER

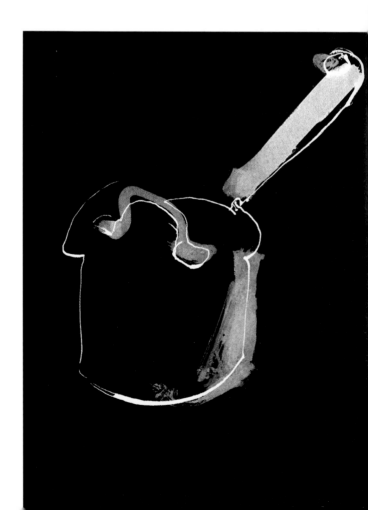

lunch and supper,
along with brunch,

...are the hardest meals to pin down, I think. A late lunch at the weekend may be the main meal of the day, whereas during the week you may have just a sandwich. Supper is sometimes a grand snack, but if you've been on the run all day it may need to be the most nourishing meal of them all. Here is a selection of recipes to cover all needs – I hope.

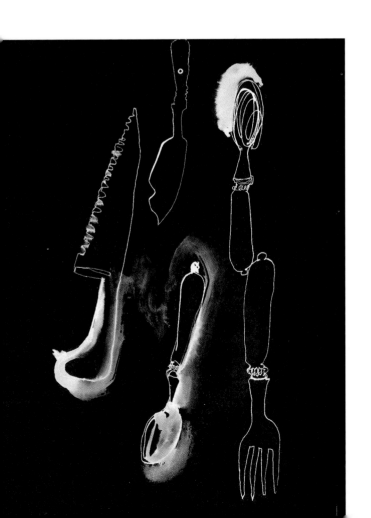

mackerel and potato salad
with dill and mustard dressing

Dill was the last herb for which I developed a liking, but it is now a firm favourite. It is great with most oily fish. Mackerel is often underrated, but this treatment will help you see it in a new light. The salad can be knocked up in less than 30 minutes, or you can make all the components up to 1 day in advance and assemble them in seconds when you want to eat. *For photographs see page 34*

FOR 4 AS A STARTER, 2 AS MAIN COURSE

mackerel	*2, about 500 g each, cleaned, heads removed*
light olive oil	*100 ml, or salad oil*
new potatoes	*600 g, cooked and halved*
large red onion	*1, peeled and finely sliced*
seed mustard	*1 tablespoon*
english mustard	*1 tablespoon*
lemon juice	*30 ml*
mayonnaise	*150 ml*
dill	*1/2 cup, roughly chopped*
salt	
black pepper	*freshly ground*

Pre-heat the oven to 220°c.

Season the stomach cavities of the mackerel with some salt and pepper and lay them in a pre-heated roasting dish, drizzle over a few teaspoons of the oil and bake for 12-15 minutes until cooked. When they are done, the flesh will pull away easily from the bone at the fattest end and will show no blood. Remove them from the oven and leave them to cool. Mix together the potatoes and onion. Stir the mustards with the lemon juice, then whisk in the rest of the oil and the mayonnaise. It should emulsify slightly. Lastly, whisk in the dill and check the seasoning.

Peel the skin off the mackerel, discard it, then remove the flesh from the bones, and break it into chunks. Mix half of the dressing with the potato salad and divide it between 4 plates. Sit the mackerel on top and pour over the remaining dressing.

feta, red onion and rosemary potato flat bread

Really, this is a pizza, but it's a little thicker than usual. I also like to serve it as a replacement for regular bread. You can use mashed sweet potato or New Zealand kumera in place of the potato if you want a richer taste.

FOR 8

potatoes	*300 g, boiled, mashed, then left to cool to just warmer than body temperature*
tepid water	*100 ml*
fresh yeast	*20 g, or 1 tablespoon dried*
strong bread flour	*approximately 500 g*
polenta meal	*150 g*
salt	*2 teaspoons*
rosemary	*12 cm branch, leaves removed and roughly chopped*
medium red onions	*3, peeled and finely sliced into rings*
feta	*200 g*
extra-virgin olive oil	*80 ml*

Mix together the mash and water in a large bowl and add the yeast. Stir well and leave to sit for 10 minutes. Add half of the flour, mix well, then put in the polenta and half of the remaining flour. Knead the dough in the bowl, adding enough extra flour to make it pliable but not sticky. Lastly, add half the rosemary, knead again, then cover the bowl with clingfilm and leave to prove in a warm place for 20 minutes. Turn the oven to 220°c. Knock back the dough. Lightly oil a 30 x 45cm baking-tray. Tip the dough on to the tray and press it out to 1/2cm thick. Sprinkle the onion slices and the remaining rosemary over the top. Crumble on the feta, drizzle with half of the olive oil and leave to rise in a warm place for 20 minutes. Put it into the oven on a low shelf and bake for 30 minutes. Move the tray to the top of the oven and cook for a further 10 minutes. Remove it from the oven and drizzle it with the remaining oil. Eat it hot or cold.

avocado, goat's cheese and chicken quesadilla

Quesadillas come from Mexico, and they're fried flour-tortilla sandwiches. I usually make them from fresh shop-bought tortillas, even though I have a genuine tortilla-maker – bought many years ago from Dean and De Luca in New York. I can make a pretty mean tortilla when I need to, but the shop ones work fine in this recipe, and it's quicker. Leftover roast chicken is good in this; otherwise roast 2 chicken breasts or legs. Serve with a crisp tomato and lettuce salad.

FOR 2

large ripe avocado	*1*
lime	*juice of 1*
spring onions	*2, finely sliced*
hot paprika	*2 good pinches*
soft flour tortillas	*4, fresh, 20cm diameter*
chicken	*300 g, cooked, roughly chopped or shredded*
goat's cheese	*100 g, or any cheese you prefer, sliced thinly*
oil	*for frying*

Cut the avocado in half and remove the stone. Scoop out the flesh with a spoon and roughly mash it with the back of a fork. Stir in the lime juice, the spring onions, the paprika, and some salt and pepper. Lay 2 of the tortillas on a worktop and divide the avocado mixture between them. Put half of the chicken on to each tortilla, then the goat's cheese. Lay the remaining tortillas on top of each and gently press them down, then turn them over. Heat 1/4cm of oil in a 24cm frying-pan and when it is hot, put in a quesadilla and cook over a moderate heat until the tortilla is golden. Gently turn it over and cook on the other side, again until golden. Remove it from the pan, cook the other one, and eat while hot.

marinated salmon and cucumber salad

FOR 2 AS A SMALL SNACK

wasabi powder	*1/4 teaspoon*
lemon juice	*20 ml*
salmon fillet	*250 g, boned and skinned, thinly sliced into 8 pieces*
cucumber	*1/3, seeded and coarsely grated*
caster sugar	*1/2 teaspoon*
spring onions	*2, finely sliced*
soy sauce	*50 ml*

This is a refreshingly cool dish that makes a perfect light lunch or early supper on a hot day. It requires minimum preparation and no cooking, so is a good one to have on hand.

For photograph see page 35

Dissolve the wasabi in the lemon juice and mix it with the salmon. Place it in the fridge for 15 minutes, stirring once. Meanwhile, mix the cucumber with the sugar and put it in the fridge. Just before serving, drain and discard the liquid from the cucumber, then mix the cucumber with the marinated salmon and spring onions and serve in small bowls, with the soy sauce drizzled over to taste.

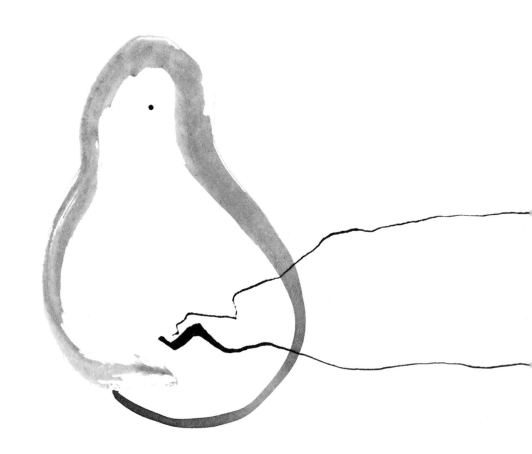

smoked eel and avocado omelette

FOR 2

smoked eel	*300 g, boned*
ripe avocado	*1*
eggs	*4*
cold water	*100 ml*
sea salt	*1/4 teaspoon*
black pepper	*a few grinds*
chives	*1 small handful, snipped*
butter	*for cooking*

This dish featured on the very first menu I created in 1986 for the original Sugar Club in Wellington, New Zealand. The combined textures of the eel and avocado, enrobed in egg, are truly delightful. Use the best smoked eel you can find, or smoked mackerel makes a good alternative.

Cut the eel into bite-sized chunks. Halve the avocado, remove the stone, peel it and cut it into bite-sized pieces. In a bowl, lightly beat the eggs, water, salt, black pepper and chives with a fork for just 5 seconds, making sure that the yolks are broken. Heat a 12cm non-stick frying-pan and add a knob of butter. Once it stops sizzling add half of the egg mixture and gently swish it around the pan. Scatter half of the avocado and half of the eel on top and cook over a moderate heat for a minute, until the egg is almost set. Fold the sides into and on top of the filling, then gently slide out the omelette on to a warm plate. Repeat with the remaining ingredients. Great eaten with toast.

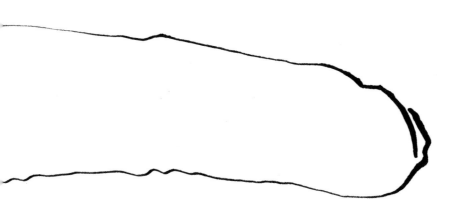

duck, grilled corn, noodle and pickled plum salad

This is a 'composed' salad, which may look difficult to achieve because the different elements all have to be made separately, but each step in itself is very simple. The advantage of a salad like this is that once you have mastered each method you can use it in other dishes, so you are constantly building up a repertoire of useful ideas. Always cook duck with its skin intact: this will keep the flesh moist – you can always remove it from the cooked bird later. Start this recipe 5 days in advance: the plums take a few days to mature.

FOR 6 GENEROUS STARTERS

oven-ready duck	*1, around 1.5 kg*
pickled plums	*9*
medium red onions	*2, peeled and finely sliced into rings*
lemon juice	*100 ml*
corncob	*1, trimmed, silk removed*
spring onions	*10, diagonally sliced into fine slivers*
egg noodles	*1 packet*
cucumber	*1/2*
carrot	*1, peeled*
sesame oil	*50 ml*
salad oil	*100 ml*

Pre-heat the oven to 190°c. Lightly season the inside and the skin of the duck with salt and pepper. Put it into a casserole dish just large enough to hold it and add 250 ml hot water, then put it into the oven and roast for 40 minutes. Remove it from the oven and prick the skin all over with a cocktail stick, which will help to release the fat, then return it to the oven for a further 45 minutes. The duck is cooked if the juices run clear when you make a small prick in the thigh. Remove the bird from the dish and allow it to cool.

As soon as the duck goes into the oven, mix the onion rings with the lemon juice and leave them to marinate for 2 hours. Lightly oil the corncob. Heat a frying-pan to smoking point and put in the corncob. Turn it so that it gradually blackens all over, but don't let it dry out. This will take around 3-4 minutes. Strip the kernels from the cob.

Cook the noodles as described on the packet and toss them in a little sesame oil to prevent them sticking to each other. Using a sharp knife or vegetable peeler, shave the cucumber and the carrot into thin ribbons.

To assemble the dish, remove and discard the fat and skin from the cooled duck. Then remove the flesh from the bones and slice it finely. Put all the other ingredients into a large bowl, plus 100 ml of the plum pickling juice, and mix together. Put mounds of the noodle salad on to plates and arrange the duck on top, dividing the leg and breast meat evenly. Drizzle over the remaining juices from the bowl.

for the pickled plums

ripe plums	*15 medium, washed, cut in half, stones removed*
cider vinegar	*200 ml*
water	*400 ml*
whole star anise	*2*
clove	*1*
sea salt	*1 teaspoon*
chilli powder	*1/2 teaspoon*
caster sugar	*300 g, unrefined*

To pickle the plums, put all the ingredients, except the fruit, into a saucepan and bring it to the boil. Warm a heatproof jar by filling it with boiling hot water for a few minutes, then drain it. Put the plums into the jar and pour on the boiling liquid and spices, then seal the jar. Once completely cool, put the jar into the fridge and leave it for at least 5 days and up to 2 months. If you can, pickle more plums than you need at once: it will not take much extra time and you'll have delicious plums on hand for other dishes.

chicken and mange tout broth
with avocado and tomato salsa

FOR 8

small chicken	*1*
medium carrots	*2, peeled and cut in half lengthways*
celery stalk	*1, cut into 4*
medium white onion	*1, peeled and finely sliced*
garlic	*2 cloves, roughly chopped*
lemon	*1, cut into quarters*
dry white wine	*300 ml*
bay leaves	*2*
salt	
black pepper	*freshly ground*
fresh oregano	*1 sprig, or 1 teaspoon dried*
mange tout	*20, finely sliced*
medium avocado	*1*
spring onions	*6, finely sliced*
lemon	*juice of 1*
large tomato	*1, ripe, cut into 1/2cm dice*

The idea for this recipe came to me from a Mexican dish I first ate years ago in San Francisco. It's a soup with a chunky guacamole. It's also delicious with 1 or 2 medium-hot green chillies, finely chopped, stirred in just before serving and a dollop of sour cream stirred in at the last minute. For a truly Mexican feel, fry some shredded soft corn tortillas in hot oil until they are crispy, then add them to the soup.

For photograph see page 35

Cut the legs off the chicken, then put them with the carcass into a deep pot with the next 7 ingredients and a teaspoon of salt. Add cold water to just cover everything and bring to the boil, skimming off any froth that rises to the surface. Reduce to a simmer and poach the chicken until it is cooked, about 30-45 minutes depending on the size of the bird. Remove the legs and carcass and leave them to cool on a plate. When the meat is cool enough to handle, pull off the skin, remove the flesh from the bones and cut it roughly into 1cm dice. Put the bones back into the stock and simmer for a further 30 minutes.

Peel and stone the avocado, cut it into 1/2cm dice and mix it with the spring onions, lemon juice, tomato, and a little salt and pepper.

Strain the chicken stock into a clean pot, check the seasoning and bring it back to the boil. Skim off any scum and add the mange tout. Boil for 20 seconds then remove from the heat. Divide the chicken flesh into 8 soup bowls and ladle some of the broth and peas on top. Add a spoonful of salsa and eat.

fried tomato chutney, ham,
walnut and cheese sandwiches

You've just run in the door, you need to be out again in 15 minutes, and you're starving. With some bottled chutney in the cupboard, ham in the fridge and a bit of bread, even if it's slightly stale, you're sorted.

FOR 2

bread	*4 slices*
butter	*120 g*
ham	*4 slices*
tomato chutney	*2 tablespoons, or any chutney will do*
grated cheese	*40 g (I like gruyère or cheddar)*
walnuts	*1 small handful, roughly chopped*

Butter the bread generously on both sides with half the butter. Lay 2 pieces down and sit a slice of ham on each, spread half of the chutney on top and sprinkle with the cheese. Lay on another slice of ham then another slice of buttered bread. Heat a frying-pan and put in three-quarters of the remaining butter. When it has melted put in the sandwiches and fry them over a moderate heat until golden. Turn them carefully and cook on the other side until golden. Remove from the pan, add the remaining butter and fry the nuts until they are also golden. Spoon them over the sandwiches and eat while hot.

broccoli, olive, mozzarella
and caramelised onion pizza

FOR ENOUGH PIZZA TO PLEASE 4 HUNGRY ADULTS

fresh yeast	*15 g, or 1 dessertspoon dried*
warm water	*500 ml*
fresh herbs	*2 tablespoons, finely chopped (rosemary, thyme, oregano)*
strong flour	*800 g*
salt	*1 teaspoon*
extra-virgin olive oil	*200 ml*
medium red onions	*4, peeled and sliced into 1|2cm thick rings*
balsamic vinegar	*100 ml*
black and green olives	*300 g, pitted*
black pepper	*freshly ground*
broccoli	*1 large head*
mozzarella	*2 balls*

You can buy a pizza base at your local supermarket, but if you have around 2 hours to spare you can easily make your own, which will be much nicer. I like a pizza base to be rolled out really thin, spread with whatever topping you choose, then baked at a high temperature until crisp. It's easier than you think!

Dissolve the yeast in the warm water in a large bowl, then add the herbs and half of the flour. Mix well with a wooden spoon. Add half of the oil, the salt and half of the remaining flour, then using your hands, begin to knead the dough, which will still be quite wet. Add more flour as you need it to produce a soft, but not sticky, dough — you may not need all of the 800 g. This should take around 10 minutes. Seal the bowl with clingfilm, and put it in a warm place for an hour, in which time the dough will increase in bulk.

Meanwhile, fry the onions in the remaining oil over a moderate heat until they have wilted and are beginning to stick to the pan. Stir in the balsamic vinegar, the olives and a few grindings of black pepper, put a lid on the pan, then stew for 10 minutes on a gentle heat. Remove the lid and cook until the vinegar has evaporated.

Finely slice the broccoli, stopping when you get to the stem. Slice or coarsely grate the mozzarella.

Turn on the oven to its highest setting. Remove the clingfilm from the bowl, and punch the dough with your fist to knock out the air. Lightly oil a 40 x 30cm baking-sheet, place the dough on top, dust it with a little flour and roll it out as thinly as you can to cover the baking-sheet. Scatter on the broccoli, then the onions and olives, lastly the mozzarella. Leave it in a warm place for 10 minutes. Bake at the top of the oven for around 25 minutes, at which point the base should be crisp and the top meltingly golden. If not, cook for up to 5 minutes more.

grilled morcilla and apples with potato tortilla

FOR 6

large potatoes	*800 g, peeled and cut into 1cm dice*
olive oil	*200 ml*
large onion	*1, peeled and sliced*
eggs	*8*
parsley	*1 small bunch, roughly chopped*
salt	
black pepper	*freshly ground*
morcilla	*750 g, cut into 1cm rings*
granny smith apples	*2-3, peeled, cored and cut into 1cm slices*

Morcilla is a Spanish black pudding, which contains rice, but if you can't get hold of it, use regular black pudding. A Spanish tortilla is a potato omelette – unlike Mexican tortillas, which are corn- or wheat-based soft pancakes – and is often best made the day before you want to eat it. However, it can be knocked up in a few minutes – if the potatoes are already cooked – and eaten while it is still hot. The amount of oil in the recipe may seem excessive, but an oily tortilla is what it's all about. If you decide it's too much, cook it in a non-stick pan.

Boil the potatoes in salted water until just cooked, then drain well. Heat half the oil in a 25-30cm pan and fry the onion until it is golden. Add the potatoes and continue to fry until they just begin to colour. While they're cooking, break the eggs into a large bowl and whisk for a few seconds, then beat in the parsley with some salt and pepper. Tip the onion and potatoes into the egg mixture and stir well. Return the pan to a high heat. Once it is hot, put in the remaining oil and, when it's smoking, carefully pour in the egg. Every 10 seconds or so, stir the tortilla, bringing the set outside bits into the centre, and gently shaking the pan. This ensures that it cooks quickly and evenly. After about 2 minutes, either turn down the heat, place a lid on the pan and continue to cook on the stove, or sit the pan under a medium-hot grill. Either method will set the uncooked eggy bits in the centre. After another minute or two, test the tortilla with a sharp knife: when it comes out clean, if a little oily, the tortilla is done. You can eat it straight away, or leave it to go cold, refrigerate and eat it the next day.

Turn the grill to maximum, and line a baking-tray with lightly oiled foil. Lay on it the slices of apple, seasoned with a little salt and pepper, and the morcilla. Grill until the apples begin to go golden then turn them and the morcilla over. Cook the same on the other side.

Cut the tortilla into 6 wedges, sit some slices of apple and morcilla on each piece. Serve a crisp salad alongside with a tangy dressing.

cherry tomato, garlic, feta and basil sauce
for pasta or gnocchi

The olive oil and garlic in this recipe may seem excessive, but as it dribbles down your chin you'll realise it's well worth it. Use a combination of red and yellow tomatoes for this – it looks great.

FOR 6 LARGE PLATES OF PASTA OR GNOCCHI

extra-virgin olive oil	*200 ml*
garlic	*15 cloves, peeled and halved*
cherry tomatoes	*500 g*
basil leaves	*1 cup, loosely packed*
feta	*250 g, roughly crumbled*

Place the oil and garlic in a saucepan and fry over moderate heat, stirring occasionally, until the garlic is golden and soft, about 6 minutes. Add the tomatoes and basil, stir well, and cook for about 3 minutes until the tomato skins just begin to burst. Add the feta and gently mix it in. Taste for seasoning, then spoon the sauce over cooked pasta or gnocchi, and eat while piping hot.

rose gordon's bacon and egg pie

My stepmother Rose makes the best bacon and egg pie in the universe. I used to love it when she made one for Saturday lunch when I was a kid – and it's almost better cold the next day. You can make your own puff pastry, but if you're in a hurry, use a good commercial ready-rolled one. Sometimes in summer Rose placed slices of garden-fresh tomatoes on top. Thanks, Rose.

FOR 6

puff or flaky pastry	*400 g*
butter	*50 g*
smoked bacon lardons	*400 g, rindless*
large white onion	*1, peeled and finely sliced*
frozen peas	*200 g*
eggs	*8*
double cream	*300 ml*
salt	*1 teaspoon*
black pepper	*1 teaspoon, freshly ground*
cheddar	*100 g, coarsely grated*

Pre-heat the oven to 180°c. You'll need a 5cm deep, 2-litre pie-dish.

Roll out the pastry on a lightly floured board to 1/2cm thick and use it to line the pie-dish. Trim off the edges, and prick the bottom with a fork 20 times. Heat the butter in a saucepan. When it has melted and is hot, add the bacon and fry it until it is beginning to colour. Put in the onions, stir well and fry until the onions begin to colour, then stir in the peas and cook for another minute. Pour this mixture into the pie shell and crack 6 eggs evenly on top. Beat the remaining eggs with the cream, salt and pepper and pour over the filling. Scatter the cheese on top and bake in the centre of the oven until the filling sets and the pastry is golden, about 40-45 minutes.

tofu, ginger, spinach and coconut curry

This curry has its roots in Thailand, and the amount of chilli you use is really up to you. Sometimes, after a particularly heavy night, a really hot curry does wonders for the system. There are many types of tofu, but for this dish use a firm one that won't break up when it's cooking. You can also buy a smoked tofu from most supermarkets, these days, and the smoky taste is great in this dish. Eat your curry with plain boiled rice, and some poppadums or crushed roasted cashew nuts for crunch. A good mango pickle, some thick plain yoghurt, and a little toasted desiccated coconut also make good accompaniments.

FOR 4

sesame oil	*50 ml*
large red onions	*2, peeled and finely sliced*
fresh ginger	*1 1/2 thumbs, peeled and finely chopped or grated*
garlic	*3 cloves, peeled and finely chopped*
red or green chillies	*2, finely sliced – keep the seeds in if you like your curry hot*
tomatoes	*3, cut into 2cm dice, or 2 tablespoons tomato purée*
lemon grass stem	*1, cut in half and flattened with the back of a knife*
kaffir lime leaves	*4 (optional)*
tofu	*400 g, cut into 2cm dice*
unsweetened coconut milk	*400 ml*
thai fish sauce	*20 ml, or 1 teaspoon salt*
spinach	*400 g, washed, larger leaves ripped in half*
coriander leaves	*1 cup*

Heat the oil in either a wok or a deep saucepan. Add the onions and fry, stirring well, until deeply coloured, then put in the ginger, garlic and chillies and fry for a further minute, stirring well. Add the tomatoes, lemon grass, lime leaves and tofu, and stir gently over a moderate heat for 1 minute so that the tofu is coated with the mixture. Add the coconut milk, then rinse out the tin with 200 ml water and pour it in. Then put in the fish sauce and bring to a simmer. Cook, uncovered, for 4 minutes, then stir in the spinach and gently toss everything together. Simmer for 2-3 minutes, taste for seasoning, and serve while hot, scattering over the coriander as you spoon it on the plates.

mussel and sweet potato fritters
with chilli and nashi salsa

I first made these fritters to be served as a canapé to passengers flying first class with Air New Zealand, and they were very popular. On the planes, though, we used New Zealand greenshell mussels, which are a lot bigger and, in my mind, tastier. Use these if you can find them: cut them into quarters once they have steamed open, and use only 10. Nashi, also called Japanese apple, is a hybrid fruit commonly grown in New Zealand, which can be replaced with either pear or apple.

FOR 4 LARGE FRITTERS

large eggs	*3, lightly beaten*
double cream	*50 ml*
thai fish sauce	*10 ml*
polenta	*4 tablespoons*
spring onions	*1/2 cup, finely sliced*
mussels	*32, steamed open and removed from the shell*
orange sweet potato	*300 g, peeled and cut into 1cm dice, then boiled until cooked*
green chilli	*1/2, seeded and finely chopped*
small red onion	*1, peeled and finely sliced*
fresh lime juice	*20 ml*
nashi	*2, cored and finely diced*
extra-virgin olive oil	*30 ml*
salt	
black pepper	*freshly ground*
cooking oil	

Mix the eggs, cream, fish sauce, polenta and half the spring onions in a bowl. Add the mussels and the sweet potato, then stir well to combine.

To make the salsa, mix together the remaining ingredients, including the rest of the spring onions, season lightly, and leave to mature for 15 minutes.

Make one fritter at a time. Heat a 15cm frying-pan and lightly brush it with cooking oil. Spoon a quarter of the mussel mixture into the centre of the pan and cook to golden brown on one side, then carefully flip over and cook for 1 minute on the other side.

Serve each fritter with some of the salsa dolloped on top.
(A dollop of crème fraîche will make it even better!)

PIC

NICS

picnics. . .
wonderful feasts
in the sun,

under a tree, in a field, at a sports game, by a river – right? Well, I've enjoyed many a sunny picnic, but some of the most memorable ones have been rather less than warm: in Sydney, July 1998, Michael and I picnicked on white bean salad and olives in a howling gale with our friends Elspeth and Charlie while their daughter Nina was blown all over the field with the cockatoos; in Richmond Park, 1992, Stephen and Marina were over from Italy and we ate cured meats and cheese hiding in the bushes with the deer and our umbrellas. When we made it back to the car we were soaked. The component common to every picnic, though, rain or shine, was a delicious array of foods.

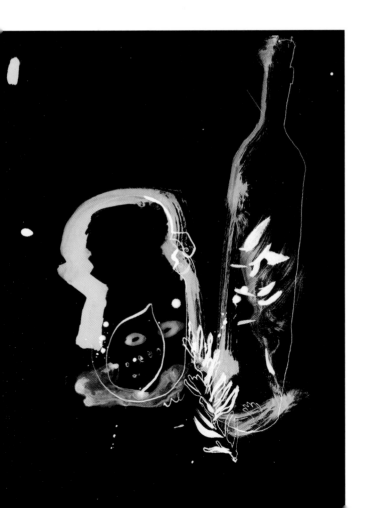

salad of spicy chicken,
coriander and peanuts with green yoghurt sauce

FOR 6

chicken legs	*3, skinned and boned*
chicken breasts	*3, skin and wing bones removed*
hot red chillies	*2, stems removed, roughly chopped*
garlic	*6 cloves, peeled*
ginger	*1 thumb, peeled and grated*
ground coriander seeds	*1 teaspoon*
cumin seeds	*1 teaspoon*
cooking oil	*100 ml*
thai fish sauce	*50 ml*
water	*50 ml*
coriander leaves	*2 cups, picked from the stems*
mint leaves	*1 cup*
spring onions	*8, roughly chopped*
garlic	*2 cloves, peeled and finely crushed*
greek style yoghurt	*300 ml*
peanuts	*1 cup, roasted and roughly crushed*

This salad will need to be kept cold so if you're taking it on a picnic, put it in a 'chilly-bin', as we call them in New Zealand. This is one of my favourite dishes, and one that I change a little each time I make it, with chunks of ripe mango or pear, either more or less chilli, or some fresh Thai basil when I can get it. It will stand up to many adaptations.

Pre-heat the oven to 230°c.

Put the chicken legs and breasts into a bowl. Place the next 8 ingredients into a blender (not a food-processor) and purée to a paste. Pour the paste over the chicken pieces, mix well, then place them in a roasting-dish. Bake for 15 minutes, then turn them over and cook for a further 15 minutes. Remove the chicken from the dish and leave it to cool. Drain the juices from the roasting-dish into a jug.

Meanwhile, put half of the coriander, the mint, spring onions and garlic into a food-processor, roughly chop, add the yoghurt and blend well, add a pinch of salt, then place in the fridge in a clean bowl.

Cut the chicken into chunks, mix it with half of the roasting-dish juices, the remaining coriander and the peanuts and mix well. Leave to chill for a few hours.

To serve, simply spoon the yoghurt mixture on top of the chicken, and you're ready.

mango, banana, cardamom and yoghurt lassi

Lassis are to be found all over India, and this is similar to one I had in 1986 in Udaipur, Rajasthan. In India they are often plain, sometimes salted, and are always a refreshing drink to accompany a spicy meal.

FOR 4

plain yoghurt	*500 ml*
cold water	*200 ml*
large ripe mango	*1, peeled, then the flesh taken off the stone, roughly chopped*
banana	*1, peeled and sliced into 8*
ground cardamom	*1/2 teaspoon*
large lime or lemon	*juice of 1*
runny honey	*100 ml*
ice cubes	*1 cup*

Put the yoghurt, water, mango and banana into a blender and purée for 30 seconds. Add the remaining ingredients, and purée for another 30 seconds. You can either drink this now, or pour it into a Thermos with a few extra ice cubes to keep it cold on the picnic.

broad bean, chilli, tahini
and pancetta salad in pitta bread

FOR 8 SANDWICHES

olive oil	*50 ml*
pancetta	*100 g, finely diced*
podded broad beans	*400 g (1.2–1.5 kg fresh broad beans)*
red chilli	*1, finely chopped*
medium onion	*1, peeled and finely sliced*
garlic	*2 cloves, peeled and sliced*
fresh mint	*2 tablespoons, chopped*
tahini	*50 ml*
balsamic vinegar	*20 ml*
small pitta breads	*8*
crème fraîche	*80 ml*

A lovely way to serve and eat this salad: the pitta bread absorbs the flavours. If you prefer, though, you could serve the salad on its own with some fresh bread on the side.

Heat the oil in a deep frying-pan and add the pancetta. Cook on a high heat until it begins to crisp, then add the beans and chilli, and sauté until the waxy skins on the beans begin to burst, stirring gently every few seconds. Add the onion and garlic and cook for a minute more, stirring well. Remove from the heat and stir in the mint, tahini and vinegar. Split open the pitta breads and stuff them with the mixture, dollop on some crème fraîche, and squeeze the sides back together. Wrap in sandwich paper.

roast carrot and parmesan risotto cakes

FOR 12 CAKES

carrots	*400 g, peeled and sliced 1/2cm thick*
onion	*1, peeled and finely sliced*
olive oil	*50 ml*
vegetable stock	*1.2–1.5 litres, simmering*
unsalted butter	*150 g*
leeks	*2, trimmed, washed and finely sliced*
garlic	*2 cloves, peeled and finely sliced*
risotto rice	*400 g*
bay leaf	*1*
fresh thyme leaves	*4 teaspoons*
tarragon leaves	*2 teaspoons*
salt	*1 teaspoon*
black pepper	*1 teaspoon, freshly ground*
medium lemons	*finely grated zest and juice of 2*
parmesan cheese	*180 g, finely grated*
semolina	*150 g*

Pre-heat the oven to 220°c.

These are good eaten straight from the oven, but they are great for a picnic too. Use the flavours here as a base, and put in whatever else takes your fancy. I've added chopped cold roast chicken to the cooled mixture very successfully. It's also a good way to use up bits of cheese, like feta, fontina or chèvre.

Place the carrots in a roasting-dish with the onion and the olive oil. Cook until golden, about 25 minutes, then finely chop or blitz in a food-processor. Heat a heavy saucepan and put in the butter, leeks and garlic. Sauté, stirring gently, until the mixture begins to caramelise. Add the rice, turn up the heat to full and fry it for a minute, stirring well. Add the herbs and seasoning, the carrots and lemon zest and juice, then mix well. Pour in enough hot stock to cover the rice by 1cm (it will bubble furiously at first) then turn the heat to low, stirring again. Once the liquid has been absorbed, add a further 250 ml of stock, stir for a few seconds and leave again for the liquid to be absorbed. Add another 250 ml of hot stock, stir well then wait until the liquid is absorbed. By now the risotto should be almost done. If it is still *al dente*, add a little more hot stock and cook for 5 minutes more. Stir in the parmesan, check the seasoning, then leave to cool completely. Divide the mixture into 12 balls, roll them in the semolina and flatten them slightly. Fry in a little more olive oil to colour on both sides, then bake for 15 minutes at 220°c. Serve with a salad and some chutney or relish, or as the starch component of a big picnic spread, with cold roast chicken, cured meats or poached fish.

smoked haddock and potato cakes

When it is of the best quality, smoked haddock is one of my favourite British products – the yellow-dyed stuff is not in consideration here! Try poached smoked haddock with soft-boiled eggs on toasted, buttered soda bread for breakfast. Brilliant. These cakes can be made any size, hungry adult to peckish child, and will keep in the fridge for up to 2 days. They are lovely with mayonnaise or tomato chutney. If you want to eat them at home, hot, have them with Hollandaise – really delicious.

FOR 8 BILLIARD-BALL-SIZED CAKES

smoked haddock	*600 g*
milk	*600 ml*
medium desirée potatoes	*1 kg, or similar floury spuds for mashing, peeled*
butter	*150 g, at room temperature*
black pepper	*1 teaspoon, freshly ground*
dill	*1/2 cup, roughly chopped*
spring onions	*6, finely sliced*
eggs	*2, lightly beaten*
flour	*100 g*
breadcrumbs	*150 g*

Pre-heat the oven to 170°c. Place the haddock in a shallow, non-reactive dish and cover it with the milk. Cover the dish with foil, then bake in the top half of the oven for 30 minutes. Peel back the foil and you will see that the fish is now sitting in frothy, smoky-flavoured milk. Meanwhile, boil the potatoes in lightly salted water until they are cooked, then drain well in a colander and mash with the butter, or force through a potato ricer or mouli. Never purée potatoes in a food-processor or you will end up with what looks like wallpaper paste. Take the haddock out of the oven and remove it from the milk. When it's cool enough to handle, remove the skin and bones and tear it into shreds with two forks. Leave the mash and the fish to cool to blood temperature, then mix the two together with the eggs, pepper, dill and spring onions. Taste for seasoning and leave to go cold. Divide the mixture into 8 equal balls and roll them in the flour mixed with the breadcrumbs, pressing them into fat columns. Heat a 2cm layer of oil in a frying-pan and, when it is hot enough, about 180°c, put in a few of the columns and cook until golden on all sides. Remove them from the pan and drain on kitchen paper. Repeat with the remaining columns.

aubergine, mozzarella, roast pepper and olive rolls

This will make 12 delicious rolls, but you could, as a variation, replace the mozzarella with a soft goat's cheese and add lots of chopped basil or parsley ... use the recipe as a starting point to make whatever you want!

FOR 4–6 AS A MAIN COURSE, 12 AS A SIDE DISH

large aubergines	*2*
salt	
black pepper	*freshly ground*
extra-virgin olive oil	*50 ml*
black olive paste	*100 g*
large red peppers	*3, roasted or grilled, peeled and cut into 4*
mozzarella	*300 g, sliced into 24*

Cut the stalk ends off the aubergines, and stand them on their heads – the flat side you just made. Slice each one downwards evenly into 8, discarding the outer 2 slices; this will leave you with 6 slices per aubergine. Season with salt and black pepper, then brush with a little olive oil and grill for 2-3 minutes each side until golden and cooked. (You can also roast them on a baking-tray at 180°c for about 15 minutes.) Leave to cool. Lay each piece of aubergine on a board and spread with some of the olive paste, a piece of red pepper and 2 slices of mozzarella. Roll up the aubergine, from the skinny end towards the fat end. Lay the rolls in a dish and leave to chill in the fridge for at least an hour to firm up.

grilled asparagus
with *jamòn serrano* and nectarine dressing

I've been to Spain several times and just adore the food there. If you go you'll be thrilled at how delicious their fantastic *jamòn* (ham) is. The Spanish are justly proud of their pork, and especially the products of the *pata-negra* (black-foot) Iberico pig. They are well worth hunting out and paying top dollar for: for the last six months of the pigs' lives, they will have been eating an almost exclusive diet of acorns. You can substitute a good prosciutto for the *jamòn* if you like. It will be almost as good.

FOR 6 AS A STARTER

fat asparagus stalks	*24*
extra-virgin olive oil	*100 ml*
large ripe nectarines	*3, or peaches, stones removed, quartered*
lemon juice	*100 ml*
salt	
black pepper	*freshly ground*
jamòn	*12 thin slices*

Lightly brush the asparagus with 10 ml of the oil and either grill it or fry it in a pan until it begins to blacken slightly. Remove it from the heat and let it cool. Put the nectarines, lemon juice and remaining oil into a blender. Purée well, then taste for seasoning. Lay the *jamòn* slices over the asparagus and pour over the dressing.

baked ricotta

This is a really easy way to transform this odd cheese into something you'd *want* to take on your picnic. This recipe was inspired by one of Katherine Smyth's – I gave her biscotti recipe in *The Sugar Club Cookbook*. She says you must only use the best ricotta and parmesan for this recipe. Some of the cheaper versions of ricotta should blush at their naming, so if you use them and they fail please don't e-mail me to complain.

FOR 8 AS A SIDE DISH

ricotta cheeses	*2 x 250 g*
fresh parmesan	*60 g, finely grated*
fresh oregano leaves	*a small handful, or a teaspoon dried*
sweet smoked paprika	*1/2 teaspoon*
salt	*a pinch*
black pepper	*1/2 teaspoon, freshly ground*
extra-virgin olive oil	*50 ml, for drizzling on top*

Pre-heat the oven to 180°c.

Cut the ricottas in half horizontally and lay them on non-stick baking parchment on a baking-sheet. Mix together the remaining ingredients, except the oil, and divide equally on top of the ricotta. Flatten it out evenly. Bake in the centre of the oven for 30 minutes, then take out and drizzle with the olive oil, and leave to go cold. That's it.

cold roast chicken breast wrapped in prosciutto
and stuffed with sage, mushrooms and sun-dried tomatoes

In early summer I like to serve this with a salad of grilled peeled red peppers and minted peas. In autumn, after a long walk in one of the parks around London, it's lovely with some sharp feta and crusty white bread.

FOR 6 ROLLS

chicken breasts	*6, skin and wing bones removed*
sage leaves	*12*
sun-dried tomatoes	*6, finely sliced*
large flat mushrooms	*3, finely sliced and sautéed in a little olive oil to soften*
prosciutto	*12 thin slices*
extra-virgin olive oil	*2 tablespoons*
black pepper	*freshly ground*

Pre-heat the oven to 220°c.

Lay the breasts flat on a board and poke a thin sharp knife horizontally into the centre of each from the rounded flat end. Gently wiggle the knife from left to right to make the cavity (being careful not to cut through the outside flesh). Divide the sage, mushrooms and tomatoes into 6 and stuff firmly into the breasts. Lay 2 pieces of the prosciutto close together on a board. Put a chicken breast on top and wrap it tightly with the prosciutto. Repeat with the remaining prosciutto and breasts.

Heat a frying-pan and when it is smoking add a little of the olive oil. Seal the breasts, in batches, and brown them all over. Place in a roasting-dish, drizzle with any remaining oil and the pan juices and roast for 20-25 minutes. Test by pushing a sharp knife through the thickest end of one breast: it should be juicy but white on the inside. Leave to cool, then place in the fridge to chill.

duck, olive and orange salad

'Succulent and juicy' was how fellow picnickers on Hampstead Heath described this salad in summer 1998.

FOR 6

duck breasts	*4 x 200 g, skin scored to help render excess fat*
oranges	*2*
black or green olives	*20–30 (150–250 g)*
extra-virgin olive oil	*30 ml*
celery	*2 stems, finely sliced*
watercress	*2 bunches, picked over and tough stems trimmed*

Pre-heat the oven to 220°c.

Lightly season the duck breasts, then brown them in a frying-pan, skin side down, over a moderate heat until the skin becomes crispish. Then place them in a roasting-dish, skin side up with a little of the rendered fat. Peel the oranges with a potato peeler or sharp knife and finely julienne the rind. Add it to the duck with the olives and toss well, then roast in the oven for 12 minutes. Remove from the oven and leave to go cold. Discard the skin if you like (I prefer to eat it!) then thinly slice the meat and place it in a bowl. Add the olives, the orange rind and the olive oil. Remove the pith from the oranges, segment them and discard the pips. Add the orange segments and the celery to the duck and gently toss together. Place the salad in a container and lay the watercress on top. When you're at your picnic spot, toss it all together and eat.

duck and ginger 'scotch quail's eggs'

FOR 12 EGGS

quail's eggs	*12*
large duck breasts	*4, skin and fat removed, leaving 600 g meat*
ginger	*1 thumb, peeled and finely grated*
spring onions	*2, roughly chopped*
salt	*1 teaspoon*
sesame oil	*20 ml*
toasted sesame seeds	*1 teaspoon*
flour	*100 g*
egg	*1, lightly beaten*
fresh breadcrumbs	*200 g*

I have loved scotch eggs from the first time I ate one: I was about six – and totally unprepared for the egg inside what I had thought was a hamburger. This quail's-egg version looks good and has about it the Asian feel I like so much. I once served these at a party as canapés with peanut sauce.

Place the quail's eggs in a small saucepan and cover them with cold water. Bring to the boil and cook for 4 minutes, then drain and refresh under cold water. Peel them carefully using your nails or a fine-pointed sharp knife to dislodge the membrane – it can be a frustrating job. Roughly chop the duck breasts into 1 cm chunks and place them in a food-processor with the ginger, spring onions, salt, sesame oil and sesame seeds. Purée for 10 seconds then scrape the bowl down; purée for 10 seconds and again scrape the bowl down; purée for another 10 seconds, at which point the meat should resemble a fine mince. Remove it from the bowl and put it in the fridge for 20 minutes to firm up. Take it out and divide it into 4 equal pieces, then divide each piece into 3. Hold one portion in the palm of your hand, flatten it out with the heel of your other hand and sit a quail's egg in the centre. Fold the mince over the egg and squeeze it into an egg-shaped 'rissole'. Repeat this with the remaining eggs and mince. If the mince sticks to your hands, moisten them with a little cold water. Roll each scotch egg in the flour, then in the beaten egg, and lastly in the breadcrumbs. Squeeze the eggs gently to ensure that the crumbs stick. Heat a deep-fryer or saucepan with at least 10 cm of cooking oil. When it reaches 170°c, put in the eggs, don't overcrowd the pan, and cook for 2-3 minutes, until they are golden brown. Remove from the pan and drain on kitchen paper. Repeat with the remaining eggs. Leave to go cold, then store in the fridge for up to 2 days.

squid, olive, tomato and garlic salad

This can be made the day before, as long as you add the olives and tomato at the last minute. If the weather is a bit nippy, serve it as soon as it's made, while it's still a little warm. It may seem a bit oily, but the oil traps a lot of flavour and is fantastic mopped up with bread.

FOR 6

medium–small squid	*1–1.5 kg, gutted, cleaned and rinsed (ask the fishmonger to do this for you if you are squeamish); cut the tube (head) in half, and try to keep the tentacles intact [see page 96 for details]*
olive oil	*250 ml*
garlic	*6 cloves, peeled*
flat-leaf parsley	*1 cup*
basil leaves	*1 cup*
coriander leaves	*1 cup*
salt	*1 teaspoon*
black pepper	*1 teaspoon, freshly ground*
large lemon	*finely grated zest and juice of 1*
best quality olives	*170 g, either green or black*
really ripe tomatoes	*6, cut into 1cm chunks*

Bring a large saucepan of salted water to the boil and plunge the squid into it. Bring back to the boil and immediately drain the squid into a colander. Don't rinse it. Put 220 ml of the olive oil into a blender and add 3 cloves of the garlic and all the herbs. Blend in short bursts until it becomes an oily paste. Add the salt and pepper, the lemon juice and zest and blend again for 10 seconds. Put the squid into a large bowl, pour on the marinade and mix well.

Finely slice the remaining garlic. Heat the remaining olive oil in a small pan and, when it's hot, add the garlic and fry it to a golden colour. Tip it on to the squid. Put in the olives and tomatoes, mix well and leave for a few minutes before serving.

grilled aubergine stack,
with vegetable relish and hummus

This is a new take on ratatouille. In this version, though, the aubergines are cooked separately and used to hold together the rest of the mixture. A big spoonful of hummus brings all the flavours together. Store these ready-made in a box to take on the picnic or, better still, assemble them once you've put the blanket down and are getting ready to eat.

FOR 4 STACKS

medium aubergines	*2 (you need 6 slices from each)*
extra-virgin olive oil	
large red onion	*1, peeled and sliced*
garlic	*4 cloves, peeled and sliced*
courgettes	*2, diced*
tomatoes	*2, skinned and diced*
sherry vinegar	*30 ml or balsamic or red wine vinegar*
salt	
black pepper	*freshly ground*
basil leaves	*1/2 cup, shredded*
chives	*1/4 cup, finely sliced*
hummus	*250 g*

Heat a heavy frying-pan or griddle. Cut the aubergine into 1 cm thick slices and brush with a little oil, then cook until soft and golden on both sides. Be careful not to let them burn – keep an eye on the heat. Leave the aubergine to cool. In a frying-pan, heat 2 tablespoons of oil, and put in the onions. Fry them until they are beginning to caramelise, then add the garlic and fry for half a minute more. Add the courgettes, tomatoes and vinegar, mix well, put a lid on the pan and cook over a gentle heat for 20 minutes, stirring occasionally. Make sure the mixture doesn't dry out or stick to the pan – add a little water if necessary to prevent this. Leave it to cool, then check for seasoning and stir in the basil and chives. To assemble the stacks, place a slice of aubergine on a plate, add an eighth of the ratatouille, another slice of aubergine, another eighth of the mixture, one last slice of aubergine, then finish with a spoonful of hummus and a drizzle of extra-virgin olive oil. Repeat with the remaining ingredients. This is good served simply with crusty bread and a tomato and mint salad.

apple, almond and stilton tart

The beauty of this tart is that it falls somewhere between savoury and sweet, which is a good thing to have on a picnic spread. I made it for the first time after visiting a smokehouse in Orford, Suffolk, where I sampled a huge variety of smoked products, from Muscovy duck to deliciously rich garlic and salmon, to Stilton. The cheese was truly delicious, and perfect with an apple. A few days later, though, the remnants were rolling about in the bottom of the fridge, so they ended up in this tart.

If you're unable to lay your hands on some smoked Stilton, use a good regular Stilton, or the fantastic Picos de Europa from Spain. Some say that this vine-leaf-wrapped blue cheese is the grandfather of Roquefort.

FOR 8–10

unsalted butter	*100 g, at room temperature*
stilton	*220 g*
caster sugar	*150 g*
ground almonds	*350 g*
eggs	*3*
medium bramleys	*3, or some other tart apple, peeled, cored and cut into eighths*
sweet shortcrust tart shell	*1 x 30 cm, baked blind*

Pre-heat the oven to 180°c.

Place the butter, stilton and sugar into a food-processor and pulse for 20 seconds, scraping down the sides as you go. Add the almonds and eggs and process for a further 20 seconds, again scraping down the sides. (If you don't have a food-processor, grate the cheese and use a wooden spoon to beat it with the butter and sugar. Gently beat in the eggs, one by one with the almonds.)

Place a quarter of the cheese mixture in the bottom of the tart shell, lay the apples evenly on top, then dollop on the remaining cheese. Bake on the middle shelf in the oven for about an hour. If the tart starts to go too brown on top, turn down the heat to 160°c. Check to see if the tart is cooked by testing the apples: they should be just soft. Leave the tart to cool completely in the tin, then put it in the fridge for at least 2 hours to firm up before taking it away in your hamper.

japanese-style tuna brochettes

FOR 8

light soy sauce	*100 ml*
sake	*50 ml, or dry sherry*
ginger	*1 teaspoon, freshly grated*
demerara sugar	*2 teaspoons*
fresh tuna loin	*800 g, sinews and skin removed, cut into 2 cm cubes*
instant wasabi paste	*1 tube, to serve*
satay sticks	*8*

This is a great way to eat fish on a picnic as the tuna stays delicious for up to 12 hours once cooked, so long as it's kept cool. Swordfish works well too, but there's something about having a little Japanese flavour on a picnic blanket that I like.

Mix together the soy sauce, sake, ginger and sugar until the sugar has dissolved, then add the tuna and stir gently. Leave it to marinate in the fridge for at least 6 hours. Drain the marinade from the tuna and discard the liquid. Divide the fish into 8 equal amounts and skewer it on the satay sticks. Heat either a grill or a heavy pan and cook for just 45 seconds on 2 sides – you want the tuna to remain rare inside. Leave it to cool before putting it into your picnic container. Serve with a little wasabi, squeezed on at the last minute.

greek-style chicken and vine-leaf roll with feta and cucumber

FOR 4 ROLLS

chicken breasts	*4, skin and wing bones removed*
salt	
black pepper	*freshly ground*
dried oregano	*1 teaspoon*
extra-virgin greek olive oil	*20 ml*
feta	*200 g, grated*
cucumber	*1/2, grated, excess moisture squeezed out*
greek-style yoghurt	*50 ml*
pickled vine leaves	*8*

These look great and keep well if made a day in advance. The vine leaves are delicious and add an unusual taste to the chicken. These days, you can buy them in larger supermarkets.

Flatten the chicken breasts to about 1 cm thick with a meat hammer or – very gently – an empty bottle. (A champagne bottle works quite well.) Season with salt and pepper and sprinkle with some dried oregano. Heat the oil in a frying-pan and sauté the breasts on both sides until they are just cooked. Mix together the feta, cucumber and yoghurt and divide it into 4. Spread it over the chicken breasts while they're still warm. Roll up each breast into a sausage shape, then wrap 2 vine leaves around each one and secure with cocktail sticks. Leave to cool, then wrap tightly in clingfilm and refrigerate for at least 2 hours. This is delicious eaten with hummus.

MARINADES
& DRESSINGS

the purpose of a
marinade

is to tenderise and add flavour to whatever you're marinating. The purpose of a dressing is to add another layer of flavour that enhances the finished dish. Here are some good examples of both.

smoked paprika and rosemary marinade

This is a simple marinade that I use a great deal in various forms. It's oil-based, which means that unlike a wine, soy, yoghurt or citrus-based marinade it will not so much tenderise as add flavour to the protein soaked in it: the oil provides a fine richness as it is gently absorbed.

This marinade works equally well with chicken legs and breasts, lamb loins, large chunks of cod fillet and salmon. I've also used it with field mushrooms, pumpkin and courgettes.

SUFFICIENT TO MARINATE 1 KG MEAT OR FISH

extra-virgin olive oil	*200 ml*
spicy smoked paprika	*1 heaped tablespoon*
rosemary	*1 heaped dessertspoon, finely chopped*
small onion	*1, peeled and finely diced*
salt	*1 teaspoon*

Mix together all of the above ingredients in a large bowl, then add the meat or fish. Leave to marinate for at least 6 hours. Wipe off and discard any excess marinade before cooking your meat or fish under a grill or on a barbecue: it might easily flare up otherwise and catch fire. If you are roasting the meat or fish, you can pour half the marinade over it for extra flavour.

nam phrik num dressing

Out of my entire repertoire of sauces and dressings, this has to be my personal favourite. Although the name suggests the chunky green mango, coriander and peanut salad from northern Thailand (which is, admittedly, where I first ate it), this dressing is actually a purée rich in a variety of tastes. I originally made it in 1986 at the first Sugar Club in Wellington. I was trying to reproduce the nam phrik salad I'd eaten in Thailand, but couldn't find green unripe mangoes. Those I located were ripe and perfumed so, I thought, why not purée the flesh and see what happens? With just a few adjustments to the original, I produced this dressing, which goes so well with fish, chicken, roast sweet potatoes, cassava chips, pumpkin and lots more besides. However, you do need a blender to make it.

FOR 8 GENEROUS MAIN-COURSE SERVINGS

lemon juice	*30 ml*
light salad oil (sunflower is good)	*250 ml*
thai fish sauce	*2 teaspoons*
limes	*zest, finely grated, and juice of 3*
very ripe mango	*1, approximately 400 g, stoned and peeled*
garlic	*1 clove, peeled*
ginger	*1 thumb, peeled and finely grated*
red chillies of medium heat	*1–2, cut into quarters*
coriander	*1 cup, washed, drained, then roughly chopped*
mint	*15 leaves*

Put all the ingredients in a blender in the same order as they are listed above, starting with the liquids. Blend for 1 minute, scraping down the sides if necessary. This dressing will keep for 2 days in the fridge, but make sure you serve it at room temperature.

lime leaf dressing

This dressing goes well with grilled duck breast, Asian-style pork and roast chicken. Or try teaming it with grilled turbot and rice, or roasted salmon fillets. The lime leaves are from kaffir lime trees, grown in Thailand. I've located them in major supermarkets and Thai and South-east Asian food stores all over the UK. When you find them, buy more than you need and freeze the remainder for up to 6 months.

You will need a blender to make this dressing as it has a high liquid content: a food-processor will merely whiz the solid ingredients around without puréeing them.

FOR 6 MAIN-COURSE SERVINGS

lime leaves	*10*
garlic	*2 cloves, peeled*
lime	*zest of 1, finely grated*
lime juice	*40 ml (2–3 limes)*
salad oil	*250 ml*
thai fish sauce	*1 teaspoon or 1/2 teaspoon salt*

Place all the ingredients in a blender and purée for 1 minute. Strain through a fine sieve to remove any fibres. This dressing will keep for up to 4 days in the fridge.

tomato, basil and ginger dressing

This light dressing goes particularly well with grilled duck, cold roast pork, poached chicken and grilled tuna. It is also good as a salad dressing or poured over grilled vegetables. Once again, you will need a blender (apologies to those of you that don't have one), and very ripe, sweet tomatoes.

FOR 6 MAIN-COURSE SERVINGS

extra-virgin olive oil	*200 ml*
ripe tomatoes	*400 g, washed and quartered*
basil leaves	*a generous handful*
ginger	*1 thumb, peeled and finely grated (optional)*
salt	*1 teaspoon*
black pepper	*1 teaspoon, freshly ground*

Place all the ingredients in a blender, in the order above, and process to a reddish-pink purée. It will take around 45 seconds. Taste for seasoning, then serve. This will keep in the fridge for 1 day, but remember to serve it at room temperature.

lemon, garlic and cumin marinade

Great with white fish, chicken and pork. It differs from the first recipe in that it uses lemon juice, which of course is acid and helps to tenderise whatever you are marinating as well as flavouring it. It's easier to make this one in a blender, although you can put it together by hand – it just takes a little longer.

SUFFICIENT TO MARINATE 1 KG MEAT OR FISH

medium lemons	*the finely grated zest and 30 ml juice of 2*
garlic	*6 cloves*
cumin seeds	*2 teaspoons, dry-roasted in a small pan and left to cool*
light oil	*200 ml, olive or sunflower work well*
salt	*1 teaspoon*

Mix all of the ingredients together in a blender for 30 seconds. Pour into a bowl and add the meat or fish. Flat white fish (brill, plaice, etc.) will need only 1-2 hours – any longer and it will start to break up. Meats can be left for up to a day. Wipe off any excess marinade and discard it, unless you are roasting the meat or fish in which case you can pour half the marinade over it for extra flavour.

fennel-seed, ginger, cardamom, coriander and yoghurt marinade

This recipe takes as its starting point the tandoori marinades of India. I like to use yoghurt-based marinades for boned lamb neck fillets, chunks of lamb, pork chops, or beef rump. It also works well with fish and vegetables (try cauliflower and courgette kebabs). The enzymes in live yoghurt act as a tenderiser, much like wine, soy and citrus juice. You can grill, barbecue or roast the marinated meat, fish or vegetables.

SUFFICIENT TO MARINATE 1 KG MEAT, FISH OR VEGETABLES

fennel seeds	*2 heaped tablespoons, lightly toasted, then cooled and crushed*
fresh ginger	*2 thumbs, peeled and finely grated*
ground cardamom	*1/2 teaspoon*
salt	*1 teaspoon*
tomato purée	*30 ml*
fresh coriander	*1 cup, finely chopped*
thick live yoghurt	*400 ml*

Combine all the ingredients in a large bowl, then add the meat or fish and mix gently. Place in a sealed container in the fridge for 6-24 hours. As with all marinades, more substantial pieces of meat or fish will need longer to marinate than smaller pieces. Wipe off and discard any excess marinade before cooking.

as I come from New Zealand, you'll have to excuse me

for thinking that the barbecue

was invented in the southern hemisphere – we spent so much time cooking family meals on ours. I was surprised to discover that the North Americans had been barbecuing for hundreds of years, as had most hunting tribes for centuries before them. Probably the first barbecue meal was a woolly mammoth steak cooked by some caveman in southern Spain. In Britain, a huge number of people thrill to the grill each summer, lining up to pay for chicken, bread rolls, charcoal and untreated wood in supermarkets all over the country. This year, why not be a little more adventurous? Try some of the following Antipodean ideas, via Asia, Greece, Spain...

tea-smoking while the barbie is burning

I do a lot of tea-smoking at the Sugar Club, and when I go visit my family in the Antipodes – everyone has an outdoors area. When the barbie is burning, make the most of it. Use the method I've given for tea-smoking salmon on page 16 and try it with any of the following:

fish fillets	*4–8 minutes depending on thickness*
chicken breasts	*6–10 minutes*
lamb loin	*6 minutes, to make it medium rare*
tofu	*about 5 minutes for a block 4cm thick*
garlic	*8 minutes, if kept as a whole head*
tomatoes	*6 minutes (then roughly chop with the garlic for a delicious salsa)*
chillies	*8 minutes*
duck breast	*6 minutes, to make it pink*
beef sirloin steaks	*3 minutes for a 350g steak, then finish it on the barbie*

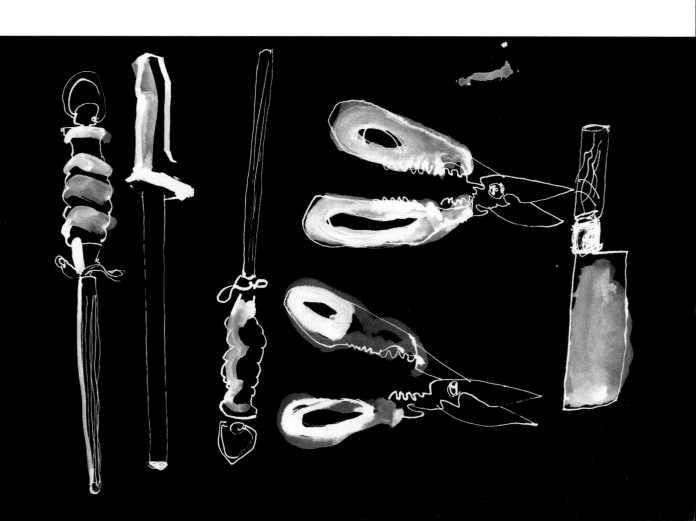

squid in sweet soy with sweet potato and bok choy

FOR 4 AS A MAIN COURSE

soy sauce	*80 ml*
mirin	*60 ml, or sweet white wine*
cinnamon stick	*1, roughly broken up*
green or red chilli	*1/2, seeds intact*
palm sugar	*100 g, or demerara sugar*
squid	*800 g small– medium, including tentacles*
sesame oil for grilling	
salt	
black pepper	*freshly ground*
medium-large sweet potatoes	*2, washed and cut into 1/2cm thick slices*
bok choy	*6–8, washed and cut in half lengthways*
	(pak choy, gai lan or chinese broccoli will work just as well)
large juicy lemons	*2, cut into wedges*

First, make the sweet soy sauce. Place the first 5 ingredients in a saucepan and bring to the boil, then turn down the heat and simmer for 5 minutes. Leave to cool then strain into a clean container.

In this recipe, the entire meal, including the green vegetables, is cooked on the barbecue. Served with some bread, or some boiled rice or noodles, this is all you need for a long summer's day meal. In order to keep squid tender, it needs to be either cooked fast and hot, or slowly simmered; here it's the former. The sweet soy caramelises almost until it burns, which is some of its appeal. *For photographs see pages 94-95*

Cut the tentacles from below the eyes of the squid and place in a bowl, then pull the guts from the head and discard. Peel off the grey membrane from the outside of the bullet-shaped heads, then cut them from the cavity towards the point and flatten them out. Scrape any remaining 'bits' still clinging to the inside of the head and discard these as well. Place the squid heads in the bowl with the tentacles and drizzle on 30 ml sesame oil and some salt and pepper.

Brush the sweet potatoes with a little sesame oil on both sides, sprinkle with a little salt, and grill on the almost-hottest part of the barbecue for around 4-5 minutes on each side, until you can push a sharp knife through them easily, but be careful not to burn them. Stack these up on top of each other to keep warm.

Toss the bok choy in a bowl with about 20 ml sesame oil and 30 ml water (this will help to steam-grill it) and toss it on the barbie for about 2 minutes, turning it to cook evenly. Move that to one side to keep warm as well. Now place the tentacles and squid heads in one layer on the barbie in the hottest place and cook without moving for 2 minutes. If the barbie begins to catch

fire drizzle on a *little* cold water. Take the squid off the grill and toss it with half of the soy sauce, then return it to the grill, this time cooking on the other side. It's inevitable that they will curl up, but that's fine, just keep turning them and make sure they don't burn too much.

To assemble, place the sweet potato and bok choy on the plates, then add the squid and tentacles, pour over the rest of the sweet soy and serve with the lemon wedges.

chorizo and potato kebabs

Chorizo, the spicy Spanish sausage, resembles a softish salami. It must be my favourite sausage as it's so versatile. You will find that some chorizo are not meant to be cooked: rather they are to be sliced and eaten as if they were a salami. You'll also find that they come in various shades of heat, from sweet and mildly spiced to fiery. Here, I team chorizo with potatoes, poke it on to a satay stick, or skewer, and grill it. The kebabs are best teamed with a chutney or relish if you're going to eat them alone, but as part of a big barbecue with plenty of salads, they don't really need it. If you soak the wooden satay sticks in cold water for at least 2 hours before using them they will be less likely to catch fire on the barbecue! *For photograph see page 94*

FOR 6 KEBABS

new potatoes *800 g washed – Jersey Royals are excellent*
chorizo *6, weighing around 180–220 g each*
satay sticks *6, or metal skewers, about 25cm long*

Boil the potatoes in salted water until cooked, then drain and refresh them. If the potatoes are large, cut them in half. Slice each chorizo into 4-6 pieces. Skewer pieces of chorizo and potato alternately on to each stick. Cook above the glowing embers of the barbecue, turning frequently, until the chorizo are beginning to brown. Chorizo are fairly oily, so you won't need to oil these kebabs before cooking them.

slightly smoky grilled quails
with ginger, mirin, basil and sesame

Quails are great to barbecue because they're easy to hold in your hands, and they'll dribble just the right amount of juice down your chin. That's a prerequisite of any barbecued meat and, anyway, you're bound to have armloads of paper napkins to hand.

FOR 4 AS A MAIN COURSE

quail	*8*
basil leaves	*a good handful, shredded, plus a little extra*
sesame oil	*50 ml*
sesame seeds	*2 teaspoons*
ginger	*1 thumb, peeled and finely minced*
garlic	*3 cloves, peeled and finely chopped*
thai fish sauce	*20 ml*
mirin	*20 ml*
vinegar	*20 ml*
demerara sugar	*1 tablespoon*
lime	*to taste*

Hold the quail in your hand, breast down, and cut out the backbone with a pair of kitchen scissors. Place the bird in a large bowl. Repeat with the others. Add the remaining ingredients and toss together, then cover with clingfilm and leave to marinate for at least 6 hours. Once the barbecue coals are glowing make them into a mound in the centre. Lay the quails, flattened out, breast side up, on the rack in a ring around this hot mound and close the lid if you have one, as this will keep the heat and some of the smoke in, but it is not essential. This will allow them to take on a smoky flavour but they shouldn't burn. Cook for 6 minutes, then open the lid, turn over the quails, close the lid again and cook for another 5-8 minutes. Test a quail by poking its thigh with a sharp knife at the thickest point. If the juices run clear, it's cooked. If they are still pink, continue to cook for a couple more minutes, then test again. If the bird is black and flaming, though, you'll be going hungry. Remove the cooked quail to a platter and sprinkle with the extra shredded basil and a squeeze of lime.

grilled tofu
with minted aubergines and courgettes

Tofu is one of those foods that divide restaurant chefs. There are those who think it's for sandal-wearers, and those who appreciate its texture, taste and subtlety. As I'm a summer sandal-wearer and as I've also eaten some of the best silken tofu to be had, I cross both camps. When you actually eat the best softest tofu, dipped in iced water and served with only soy sauce and spring onions, then you realise what a delicious thing it can be. For grilling and frying though, you need a more firm tofu that won't break up as you handle it, and this is the type most health food shops stock. Full of protein, made from soy beans (please avoid genetically modified soy beans), it's a fantastic vegetarian meat replacement, and as it is so subtle, it readily absorbs any flavours you marinate it with. Here the tofu is grilled plain, using the flavours of the vegetables to 'dolly it up', but it's also good brushed with the sweet soy from the recipe on page 96 for the last minute of its cooking, or any of the marinades from that section.

FOR 4

tofu	*500 g, sliced into 8 equal pieces, 1–2cm thick*
sesame oil	*for cooking*
large aubergines	*2, sliced into rings 1cm thick*
large courgettes	*3, sliced into rings 1cm thick*
large red onion	*1, peeled and sliced into 1|2cm rings*
mint leaves	*1 large handful, roughly chopped*
spring onions	*6, finely sliced*
light soy sauce	*30 ml, or tamari*
large lemon	*juice of 1*
toasted sesame seeds	*2 teaspoons*

Pat the tofu dry with a cloth and brush it with some sesame oil. Brush the aubergines and the courgettes with oil too, but not the onion. Make sure the barbecue embers are glowing red and lay the tofu at the outside of the grill – still in a hot place, though – then put the onions, aubergines and courgettes towards the middle in a single layer. Cook everything without turning until coloured on one side, then turn and continue to cook until you can push a small knife easily into the courgettes and aubergines. Remove the vegetables and place them in a large bowl or on a large platter. Add the mint, spring onions, lemon juice, soy and sesame seeds, and gently toss together. Serve with the grilled tofu straight off the grill.

duck marinated in thyme and cumin

A simple marinade can make all the difference to a piece of barbecued meat and I like a little sweetness in mine: the sugars caramelise on the heat, and the combination of sweet with smoky is irresistible. With the high amount of fat in duck, you must keep an eye on them on the barbecue: a major flare-up could turn it into a furnace – but it's unlikely to happen.

FOR 6

duck	*1 x 2 kg*
salt	*2 teaspoons*
honey	*50 ml, or maple syrup*
fresh thyme	*1 small bunch, finely chopped, or 2 teaspoons dried*
ground cumin	*3 teaspoons*
cider vinegar	*50 ml*

Remove the legs from the duck and cut each in half at the knee joint. Remove the breasts from the carcass and trim off any excess fat. Bring a large saucepan of water to the boil and put in the breasts and legs. Cook for 2 minutes, then remove them from the pan and lay them on a board. Using a sharp knife or cocktail stick, prick the skin all over to help release some of the fat. Pat the duck pieces dry with absorbent kitchen paper and lay them in a bowl. Mix together the remaining ingredients into a loose paste and pour it over the duck, then rub it in well. Leave to marinate for at least 3 hours, and up to 24, turning every now and then.

Once the barbecue is hot enough, wipe the excess marinade from the duck and place it on the barbecue. After 3 minutes turn it and keep an eye on it for flare-ups. Keep turning the meat from time to time. The breasts will take 8-10 minutes to become medium rare, while the legs may take up to 25 minutes. A minute before they're ready, brush them with some of the marinade for extra flavour.

whole baked snapper with yoghurt, olives and thyme

This is something you could cook in the embers of a barbecue while you're having the 'picky' first course. (You can also bake it in the oven.) Serve it with lots of baby potatoes, tossed with olive oil or butter, and a big green salad. Use any fish that takes your fancy and, allowing for the weight of the bones, you will need around 400 g per person for a main course. The cooking time will vary, according to the thickness of the fish and its overall weight, so keep your eye on it.

FOR 6

whole snapper	*2 x 2.5 kg, scaled and gutted*
yoghurt	*400 ml*
lemon juice	*50 ml*
thyme	*1 handful, roughly chopped, stems and all*
sea salt	*2 teaspoons*
black pepper	*2 teaspoons, freshly ground*
green olives	*250 g with or without stones*
large red onion	*1, finely sliced*

Cut 3 gashes at an angle in the thickest part of the fish, on both sides, to allow the marinade to work effectively. Trim off any fins or sharp bits with scissors. Mix together the yoghurt, lemon juice, half of the thyme and all the seasonings and rub it into the fish, especially the cuts and the stomach cavity. Cover with clingfilm and place in the fridge, turning every 3 hours for 12-24 hours.

Get the barbecue embers hot, or the oven to 220°c. Mix together the olives, onion and the remaining thyme. Drain the marinade from the fish and stuff the olive mixture into its stomach. Secure it with a satay stick or skewer to keep the olives in. Lightly oil a large double thickness sheet of baking foil and wrap the fish tightly in it, being careful not to rip it. Place the parcel in the embers of the barbecue or in a pre-heated roasting-dish and cook for 1 hour, turning once half-way through. Test to see if it's cooked by peeling back some foil at the thickest part. The flesh should be opaque, not raw. Cut open the foil with scissors then scoop out the flesh and stuffing with a spoon and fork. Eat immediately.

lamb and lime-leaf burgers

The humble hamburger transformed into a mini South-east Asian feast. The lime leaves I use here are kaffir lime leaves, imported from Thailand. They usually come looking as though two leaves are stuck together, but in fact this is one leaf. I have several times used unsprayed Sicilian lemon leaves to much the same effect – they also went really well with pork mince. Once made, the burger mixture will keep chilled for up to 2 days, so plan ahead and you could take this in a chilly-bin on a hike through the Pennines and cook it up for dinner!

FOR 10 BURGERS

lime leaves	*15*
eggs	*2*
thai fish sauce	*40 ml*
lamb	*2 kg, finely minced (as lean as you want)*
cornflour	*150 g*
salt	*1 teaspoon*
garlic	*2 cloves, peeled and finely chopped*
medium red onion	*1, peeled and finely chopped*

Place the lime leaves, eggs and fish sauce in a blender and purée for 20 seconds. Scrape down the sides of the jug and purée for a further 20 seconds. Pass the contents through a sieve to remove fibres and stem, and mix with all the remaining ingredients. Shape into 1 cm thick patties, lay them on a tray and put them in the fridge until you need them.

Cook over a moderate-high heat for about 3 minutes on each side to produce a succulent aromatic burger. Serve in a bun, with lavish amounts of fresh coriander leaves, thick yoghurt, sliced green tomatoes and peanut butter.

chicken and lemon-grass brochette
with sesame dressing

The Vietnamese make a wonderful dish of minced prawn and pork wrapped round sugar-cane and grilled on a brazier. This is a more accessible version of that idea – when did you last see a piece of young sugar-cane? You could make the brochettes very small, dip them into a beer batter and deep-fry them until they are crispy, then serve them as canapés.

FOR 4 AS A STARTER

FOR THE BROCHETTES

chicken mince	*500 g*
egg white	*1*
spring onions	*1 bunch, roughly chopped*
coriander leaves	*1/2 cup*
thai fish sauce	*4 teaspoons*
sesame oil	*1 teaspoon*
ginger	*1 thumb, finely grated*
cornflour	*3 tablespoons*
sesame seeds	*2 teaspoons*
lemon grass	*8 long stems*

FOR THE DRESSING

lime or lemon juice	*80 ml*
unrefined caster sugar	*1 teaspoon*
toasted sesame seeds	*4 tablespoons*
sesame oil	*50 ml*
salad oil	*100 ml*
spring onions	*1/4 cup, finely sliced*

FOR THE BEER BATTER

plain flour	*190 g*
salt	*1 teaspoon*
brown sugar	*1 teaspoon*
baking powder	*1 teaspoon*
beer	*450 ml*

Put all of the brochette ingredients, except the lemon grass, into a food-processor and purée for 30 seconds. Scrape down the bowl and purée for another 10 seconds. Put the mixture in the fridge for at least 30 minutes to firm up.

Make the dressing while the chicken is in the fridge. Whisk all of the ingredients together until the sugar is dissolved. It's fine to whisk the spring onions – they'll release more flavour that way.

Divide the mince into 8 even-sized portions. Cut the base of the lemon grass 1/2cm from the bottom. Lightly smash its lower stems to bruise them. Spread a portion of mince on the palm of your hand and lay a stem on it. Squeeze lightly to surround the stem evenly, and repeat with the rest of the mixture. You can now either grill, shallow fry or barbecue the brochettes. If you want to deep-fry them, stir the dry ingredients together for the batter and then whisk in the beer making sure you have no lumps. Let the batter rest for 10 minutes before using. Drizzle over the dressing, and serve with a cucumber or green papaya salad.

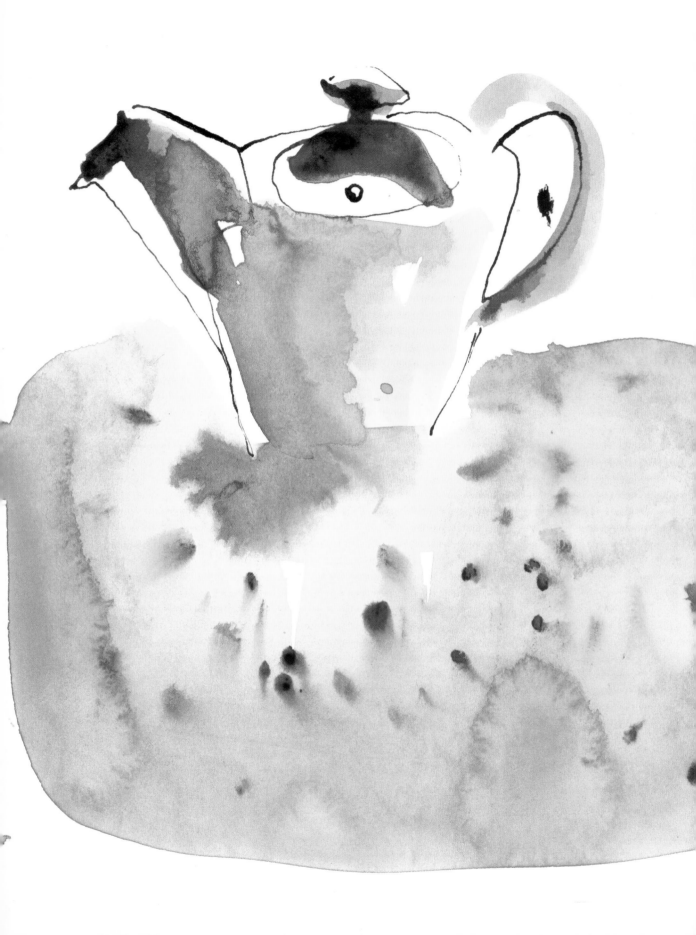

THE TEA TROLLEY
&PUDDINGS

to me,
the tea trolley

symbolises all the hours we spent as kids at our grandmother's house in Cavendish Square in Wellington, New Zealand. Gran, Molly Gordon, would have her beautiful wooden tea trolley with its funny wooden wheels always at the ready next to the stove in her kitchen supporting 4-6 jars of assorted biscuits and slices. When we heard the clacking of the wheels as it began its journey across the kitchen floor, we would all hope that our own particular favourite was going to be on board that day! I have two tea trolleys of my own now, and whenever they begin their own journey across my kitchen floor I never fail to remember Molly as an inspiration.

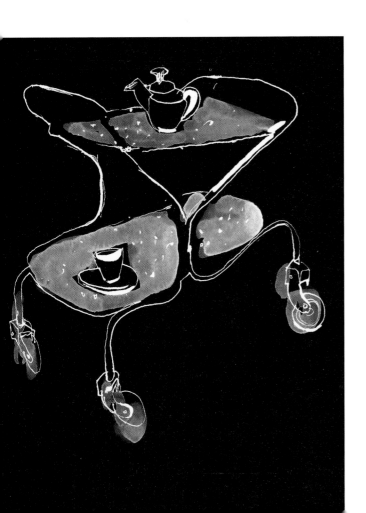

cashew and muscatel scones

I'm a huge fan of the 'cream tea', whether it be with clotted cream, crème fraîche or regular whipped cream and this recipe is a current favourite. So long as I have a fruity jam, a soft scone and something creamy to go with it I'm happy. When I was a kid, we often had savoury scones: my father added some chopped onion, parsley and a good pinch of cayenne pepper to half of the scone dough. Muscatel raisins are dried muscat grapes and taste like a chewy mouthful of port. You can generally buy them at good health-food shops, some cheese shops and delicatessens. If you can't get hold of them, though, use any plump raisins and soak them before use in a good slug of muscat or port. *For photograph see page 110*

MAKES 12 SCONES

flour	*550 g*
salt	*a pinch*
caster sugar	*2 teaspoons*
baking powder	*6 level teaspoons*
butter	*70 g, cut into small dice*
toasted cashew nuts	*100 g, roughly chopped*
muscatels	*100 g, off their stem, stoned if necessary*
milk	*375 ml, plus a little extra*

Pre-heat the oven to 220°c.

Sift the flour, salt, sugar and baking powder into a bowl, then rub in the butter with your fingers until it resembles bread-crumbs. Mix in the cashews and muscatels, then add the milk and mix quickly to a soft dough. Gently knead it for half a minute in the mixing bowl or on a lightly floured worktop. If the dough is sticky, add a little more flour. Divide the dough into 12 pieces and flatten each piece into a small crumpet shape. Place on a lightly floured baking tray, brush the tops with a little milk and bake for 15-20 minutes, until the scones have risen well and are golden on top. (I was told once that if all your scones touch each other, they will rise better, something to do with community spirit.)

emma robinson's muffins

In 1996 my old friend Emma, her husband Paul O'Brien and their daughter Vita came to live with us in London for a wee while before heading back to New Zealand. Some mornings we woke up to smell muffins baking and knew a good day was beginning. New Zealand has a great muffin culture: they're usually healthy and packed full of tasty bites – although you *can* make them with big chunks of chocolate and dried figs, which aren't so easy on the waistline. This is Emma's recipe. *For photograph see page 111*

MAKES 10-12 MUFFINS

flour	*250 g*
baking powder	*2 teaspoons*
bicarbonate of soda	*1/2 teaspoon*
salt	*a pinch*
runny honey	*50 ml*

FOR THE FLAVOURINGS – CHOOSE ONE COMBINATION

100 g grated cheddar and 1/2 teaspoon paprika
or 1 sliced ripe banana, 120 g roughly chopped nuts, and a pinch of nutmeg
or 1 cup berry fruit, fresh or frozen, blueberries and raspberries are great
or 1 grated apple, skin included, 50 g sultanas and 1/2 teaspoon cinnamon
or 120 g chopped dates, the finely grated zest of 1 orange and 20 g poppy seeds
or 100 g desiccated coconut, 40 ml cold milk and the grated zest of 1 lemon

egg	*1, lightly beaten*
yoghurt	*200 ml*

Preheat the oven to 180°c. Heavily grease and flour your muffin tins, unless you have some non-stick tins.

Sift together the first 4 ingredients, then stir in the honey. Stir in your choice of flavouring, then fold in the egg and the yoghurt. Don't mix too heavily: the final batter should look slightly uneven – if you make it too smooth the recipe doesn't work as well. Spoon the mixture into the muffin tins, filling them to the top; they will rise but shouldn't spread far. Bake for 15-20 minutes, depending on the flavouring you have chosen: the more moist the mixture, the longer it will take to cook. The muffins are ready when a thin knife inserted into them comes out clean.

mum's sesame-muesli slice

My mother Timmy and my step-dad Clyde Ludwig run a café in Queensland, Australia. Here Mum makes all the cakes, biscuits and almost everything else too. These crunchy muesli slices go down a treat with everyone, and Mum says you can use whatever dried fruit takes your fancy, but do include some mixed peel and crystallised ginger.

MAKES 32

butter	*100 g*
runny honey	*120 ml*
golden syrup	*120 ml*
brown sugar	*180 g*
bicarbonate of soda	*1 heaped teaspoon*
assorted chopped dried fruits	*180 g – apricots, mango, crystallised ginger, sultanas, dates, mixed peel, etc.*
desiccated coconut	*75 g*
muesli	*230 g*
self-raising flour	*190 g, sifted*
sunflower seeds	*40 g*
sesame seeds	*40 g*

Pre-heat the oven to 180°c. Grease a shallow 24cm square cake tin (or something similar).

Melt the butter, honey, golden syrup and sugar together in a large saucepan. Stir in the bicarbonate of soda and the dried fruits, cook over a moderate heat until the mixture froths up. Leave to cool for 15 minutes. Mix in the coconut and muesli, then add the flour and half the sunflower seeds. Mix really well, then press into a 24cm square cake tin lined with non-stick baking parchment. Sprinkle the sesame seeds and remaining sunflower seeds on top. Bake for 25-30 minutes, at which point it will be caramelised and bubbly. Remove it from the oven and leave to sit for 5 minutes, then cut into 3 x 6cm pieces with a sharp knife, as when it cools it becomes too hard to cut. Place in the fridge until it goes cold (Mum's cooking tip – don't ask me why) then remove from the tin and store in airtight containers. They will keep for 4 weeks.

double chocolate nut cookies

When I used to watch *The Brady Bunch* on television, Alice the housekeeper was always making cookies for the kids. In New Zealand we only ate biscuits and I always wondered what the difference was. Now I know: cookies always have a pinch of salt in them. This is the recipe I've evolved from many trials to produce flat, crisp cookies with hard chunks of nut and chocolate inside. Use whatever nuts you prefer, and if you only have one type of chocolate, then just use that. *For photograph see page 110*

FOR 20 COOKIES

unsalted butter	*125 g, at room temperature*
caster sugar	*70 g*
demerara sugar	*70 g*
egg	*1*
flour	*140 g*
bicarbonate of soda	*1/2 teaspoon*
salt	*a pinch*
dark chocolate	*60 g, cut into rough chunks*
white chocolate	*60 g, cut into rough chunks*
roughly chopped nuts	*80 g – I like to use pecans, peanuts or toasted hazelnuts*

Pre-heat the oven to 170°c.

Cream together the butter and the sugars, then beat in the egg. Sift together the flour, bicarbonate of soda and salt, and mix in. Stir in the chocolates and nuts. Place heaped teaspoonfuls of the mixture on greaseproof-lined trays, leaving a good amount of space between each one. Bake for 6-8 minutes, until tan-coloured and puffy, then take out the tray and bang it on a worktop to knock out the air. Return it to the oven for another 6-8 minutes until the cookies are golden brown. Take out of the oven, and again bang the tray on a worktop. Leave the cookies to cool on the tray, then store in airtight jars for up to a week.

cold chocolate and gingernut mousse with raspberries

This dessert is deceptively easy to make, but the taste is utterly decadent and rewarding. I often make it with Amaretti biscuits in place of the gingernuts, although ginger and raspberries go really well together.

FOR 8-10

powdered gelatine	*1 tablespoon*
warm water	*80 ml*
egg yolks	*5*
vanilla essence	*1 teaspoon*
unrefined caster sugar	*150 g*
milk	*400 ml*
bitter chocolate	*200 g, grated*
gingernut biscuits	*150 g, ground to coarse crumbs in a food-processor*
raspberries	*350 g*
cream	*400 ml, lightly whipped*

Sprinkle the gelatine over the warm water and stir until it has dissolved. Whisk together the egg yolks, vanilla essence and sugar until they are light and fluffy. Bring the milk to the boil, then whisk it into the egg yolks. Return it to the pan and cook over a moderate heat until it thickens, about 4 minutes, stirring continuously. Don't let it boil or it will curdle. Take it off the heat and add the dissolved gelatine, stir well, then add the chocolate and gingernuts and again mix well. Pour into a 20 cm ring mould, previously rinsed with cold water, then put it in the fridge to set for at least 4 hours. To serve, dip the ring mould briefly into hot water, then invert it on to a plate and shake out the mousse. Fill the centre with raspberries and serve lashings of whipped cream on the side.

molly's caramel shortbread

Molly Gordon died in 1996, aged ninety-seven, and she is much missed by all the remaining family. She was a huge inspiration to me, my siblings and countless others. Her regular shortbread was always popular, and she'd have lots of it in her biscuit jars. However, the discovery of a newly made batch of this was the best thing in the world! My sisters and I could eat it till the cows came home, and we often did. At the Sugar Club in Soho, we serve this on our plate of biscuits and chocolates, and it's good to know that it's still appreciated. Thanks to Stephen Latty for the photo of Molly.

MAKES ABOUT 42 FINGERS

condensed milk	*1 x 397 g tin*
unsalted butter	*250 g, at room temperature, plus an extra tablespoonful*
caster sugar	*150 g*
cornflour	*150 g*
flour	*300 g*

First make the caramel. Put the tin of condensed milk in a deep saucepan and cover it with water. Bring to the boil, then reduce the heat and put on the lid. Leave it to simmer rapidly for 2 hours. Cool it down completely before you open the tin to find a golden sticky caramel. Once cooked, a tin of caramelised condensed milk will keep in the fridge for 2 weeks.

Turn the oven to 170°c. Cream the butter with the sugar until it is light and fluffy. Sift together the flours. Mix the two together, then gently knead the dough until it comes together in a firm ball. Line a 20 x 30cm baking-tin with nonstick baking parchment. Roll out two-thirds of the dough to fit the tin and lay it inside, pressing it neatly into the edges. Spread three quarters of the condensed-milk caramel evenly over the base. Crumble out the remaining third of the dough over the top of the caramel.

Bake for 20 minutes. The caramel should have bubbled up a little among the dough, and the top of the shortbread should be golden. Leave it to cool in the tin for 5 minutes before cutting it into 3 x 5cm fingers. Leave it to cool completely in the tin, before removing it to store in an airtight jar or tin. As for the remains of the caramel, you could spoon it over some ice cream and some ripe bananas for a gooey dessert.

lemon, marzipan and almond cake

This cake is incredibly simple to make. It's similar to pound cake and goes well with strong espresso. In late summer I love it with raspberries, but it's just as good with whipped cream with lots of vanilla sugar folded through it. Any left overs will keep for 2 days in an airtight tin. *For photograph see page 110*

FOR 6-8 PEOPLE

eggs	*4*
light demerara sugar	*280 g*
unsalted butter	*140 g, at room temperature*
vanilla extract	*1 teaspoon*
flour	*220 g*
baking powder	*2 teaspoons*
lemons	*finely grated zest of 2*
cold water	*170 ml*
ground almonds	*200 g*
marzipan	*100 g*
flaked almonds	*150 g*
icing sugar	*65 g, sifted*

Pre-heat the oven to 180°c. Line a 30cm cake tin with non-stick baking parchment.

Put the first 4 ingredients into a food-processor and blitz for 1 minute. Sift the flour with the baking powder and add it, with the lemon zest, to the processor. Blitz for 10 seconds, then scrape the sides of the bowl and add the water, ground almonds and marzipan. Blitz for 1 minute, scrape the sides and blitz for 15 seconds more. Pour the batter into the cake tin and bake in the middle of the oven for 25 minutes. Then mix the flaked almonds with the icing sugar, sprinkle them on top of the cake and bake for a further 15-20 minutes. When the cake is done, a skewer inserted into it should come out clean. Leave it to cool before removing it from the tin.

macadamia and lemon myrtle biscotti

This recipe is based on Katherine Smyth's recipe, which first appeared in *The Sugar Club Cookbook*. My sister Tracey and her partner Roe now make these biscuits commercially in Bangalow, Australia for their company Wildbite. Tracey and I came up with the combo in Wanganui in 1997 when we were visiting our father Bruce. Our middle sister Donna had just spent a few months picking macadamia nuts, a backbreaking job, so they came from her. Lemon myrtle is a native Australian tree, and you can readily buy the powdered leaves there, but in England it may be easier to find dried ground lemon verbena. Either way the biscotti are delicious!

MAKES APPROXIMATELY 60 BISCOTTI

flour	*500 g*
caster sugar	*500 g*
lemon myrtle	*2 tablespoons – or lemon verbena powder*
baking powder	*1 tablespoon*
eggs	*5, lightly beaten*
macadamia nuts	*500 g*

Pre-heat the oven to 180°c.

Mix the flour, sugar, lemon myrtle and baking powder together in a large bowl. Add half of the beaten egg and mix well. Then add half of the remaining egg and mix again. Now add the rest a little at a time until the dough takes shape but isn't too wet. You may not need to use all of the egg. Add the nuts and mix well. Divide the dough into 4 and roll it into sausage shapes about 3cm in diameter. Place them on non-stick baking parchment on baking-trays, at least 8cm apart. You may find it easier to wet your hands when making the rolls to prevent the dough sticking to them. Lightly flatten the 'sausages' and bake until they are golden brown, approximately 20-30 minutes. Remove from the oven, turn down the temperature to 140°c, and leave them to sit for 10 minutes to cool and firm up. Using a sharp knife, cut the biscotti at an angle into 1cm thick slices and lay them on the baking-trays. Return them to the oven and bake for 10 minutes then turn over all the biscotti and bake until they are pale golden, approximately 10-15 minutes. Once they are done, remove them from the oven and cool them on cake racks, then store in airtight jars.

ginger crème caramel

The addition of ginger to crème caramel is a match made in culinary heaven. The creaminess combined with the refreshing bite of ginger is fantastic. It is a lovely dessert in summer or winter and makes a great addition to afternoon tea with a cup of Lady Grey tea.

MAKES 6

caster sugar	*400 g*
water	*100 ml*
milk	*600 ml*
double cream	*400 ml*
stem ginger	*80 g, finely sliced*
eggs	*7*

Pre-heat the oven to 170°c.

First make a bain-marie: fill a roasting-tin with 3cm hot water and place it in the oven on the middle shelf. Now bring half of the sugar and all the water to the boil in a saucepan and continue to boil until it caramelises. Do not stir or the caramel may crystallise. When the caramel has turned a dark golden colour, pour it very carefully into the ramekins and leave it to set. (A handy hint: to clean the saucepan, put boiling water into it and boil for a few minutes to dissolve any caramel left behind.) Put the milk, cream and ginger into a saucepan and slowly bring it to the boil. While you're waiting, whisk together the eggs and the remaining sugar for 30 seconds. When the cream comes to the boil, pour it slowly into the egg mixture while whisking gently then divide it among 6 x 300ml ovenproof ramekins. Sit them in the bain-marie and pour in more hot water to come three-quarters of the way up their sides. Cook for 35 minutes, then test them by inserting a thin knife into the centre: it should come out clean but if it doesn't cook them for 3-5 minutes more and test again.

Take the ramekins out of the bain-marie and leave them to cool before covering them and placing them in the fridge to firm up over at least 3 hours.

To serve, run a blunt knife around the sides of each ramekin then gently shake it from side to side. Invert it on a plate and tip out the crème caramel with the syrup.

passionfruit parfait

Parfait is the 'ice cream' you can make when you don't have an ice-cream machine – plus it's a lot cheaper than ice cream. It is crucially important, however, that you get your sugar syrup to the right temperature. This might take some practice, but it's well worth it. You can either pour the finished parfait into a loaf tin and serve slices of it, or freeze it in a plastic tub and scoop out balls. Try replacing the passionfruit with uncooked berry purée, cooked rhubarb purée, or puréed very ripe figs or cantaloupe melon. *For photograph see page 110*

FOR 10-12 VERY GENEROUS PORTIONS

caster sugar	*500 g*
water	*150 ml*
egg whites	*5*
icing sugar	*100 g*
fresh passionfruit pulp	*450 ml (18 – 24 juicy fruit)*
double cream	*700 ml*

Put the caster sugar and water into a small saucepan, turn the heat on full, and stir until the sugar has dissolved. Then take out your spoon and boil rapidly for 3-4 minutes, at which point the syrup should be thicker and the bubbles larger and fewer. Meanwhile, beat the egg whites with an electric beater until soft peaks form (you can do this by hand, but it can become tiring) then stop beating. Once the syrup is ready, start beating the whites again and, slowly but steadily, pour the syrup on to the meringue. You now have what is known as 'Italian meringue'. Continue beating the meringue until it has cooled slightly, then stop and leave it to cool completely. It should look very white and glossy, and be very stiff. If, however, it looks wet, sloppy and flat, you may not have cooked the syrup long enough. If, on the other hand, a lump of candy is stuck to the beater, you have overcooked it. Try again. Now mix the icing sugar into the passionfruit pulp and strain it through a fine sieve, to remove as many seeds as you like – I always keep in half, for the texture as well as the visual effect. Once the meringue is completely cold, gently mix the passionfruit into it. Beat the cream to form firm but not stiff peaks, then fold it thoroughly into the meringue. Pour into whatever container you have chosen, and freeze. It will be ready to eat within 6-8 hours and will keep for 4 weeks.

poached peaches with cream

When peaches are in season and at their best, a poached one has to be the most perfect dessert. The way to bring variety to it, though, is to flavour the poaching liquid in different ways. Follow the method outlined below, then try different flavours depending on your mood.

FOR 6

white wine *800 ml*
caster sugar *500 g*
vanilla pod *1, split down the middle*
lemon *peel of 1*
peaches *6, soft enough to give slightly when you squeeze them gently*

Place all the ingredients, except the fruit, in a saucepan just large enough to hold all the peaches at once, and bring to the boil, then simmer for 5 minutes. Bring a kettle of water to the boil. Score a cross in the skin on the bottom of the peaches, as you would to peel a tomato, being careful not to cut into the flesh too deeply. Gently place the peaches in the pan with a slotted spoon. There should be enough liquid to allow the fruit to float, but if not pour in some boiling water from the kettle. Lay a circular piece of non-stick baking parchment, cut to the same size as the pan, on top of the fruit. Bring the liquid back to the boil, then gently simmer for 15-35 minutes: the cooking time will vary according to the size and ripeness of the fruit. The peaches are cooked when a skewer goes easily through to the stone. Have ready a bowl of iced water and gently lift out the fruit with a slotted spoon, then place them in the water. Leave for a few minutes then peel off the skin with your fingers. (Occasionally you'll find some won't budge, so you'll be eating the skin too!) Once the peaches are peeled, return them to the syrup and leave them to cool. I like to eat peaches done like this with whipped cream, and if you have some really sweet ripe berries, mash them with a fork, and spoon them over as well.

VARIATIONS

Replace the sugar with a light honey, add the juice and zest of 2 lemons and 1 teaspoon of lightly toasted, crushed fennel seeds.
Use red wine, add 3 star anise and 1/2 red chilli, seeds intact.
Use golden syrup instead of sugar, and orange instead of lemon.
Once the peaches are cooked, add 2 tablespoons of rose-water to the syrup.

pear, pistachio and prune tart

This looks like a lot of steps to make a tart, but you do need to cook the pears and to rehydrate the prunes before you bake them. You could easily substitute almonds for the pistachios, and you can omit the rose-water, but it adds a Middle Eastern touch to the dessert.

FOR 6-8

large ripe cooking pears	*3, peeled, cored and quartered*
honey	*100 ml*
cinnamon stick	*1*
lemon	*peel of 1*
smallish pitted prunes	*12*
unsalted pistachio nuts	*230 g, shelled plus 50 g extra for garnish, lightly toasted*
icing sugar	*180 g*
butter	*180 g, at room temperature*
eggs	*2*
flour	*2 tablespoons*
sweet shortcrust tart shell	*1 x 24–30cm, baked blind*
rose-water	*4 teaspoons*

Pre-heat the oven to 180°c. Place the pears in a small saucepan with the honey, cinnamon and lemon peel. Add enough cold water to cover, then simmer gently, with a lid on, until the pears are just cooked. Remove them with a slotted spoon and allow them to drip dry on a cake rack. Bring the liquid back to the boil and add the prunes, simmer for 5 minutes then leave them to cool in the liquid. Once cooled, remove them to a plate and reserve the liquid.

Put the pistachio nuts into a food-processor with the icing sugar and grind to a fine powder. Add the butter and eggs and process for 10 seconds, then scrape the sides, add the flour and process again briefly. Spread this mixture in the tart shell (it should make a 1cm-deep layer). Lay the pear segments and prunes in a pattern on top of the filling, pressing them in gently. Bake in the middle of the oven for about 40 minutes. It is cooked when a skewer placed in the centre of the filling comes out clean.

Meanwhile, remove the cinnamon from the syrup and bring it to the boil. Reduce until it has thickened, then add the toasted nuts and rose-water and turn off the heat. When you serve the tart, drizzle some of the nutty sauce over it.

roast pear with cinnamon and honey

This is a good way to cook pears – it must be their natural sweetness that gives them such a golden glow when they are done. Serve with custard, mascarpone or thick cream.

FOR 6

ripe cooking pears	*6, cored*
cinnamon sticks	*2, snapped in half*
runny honey	*200 ml – use one that isn't too heavy or dark*
white wine	*450 ml*

Pre-heat the oven to 180°c.

Using an apple-corer or melon-baller, remove the cores from the pears. Sit them on top of the cinnamon sticks in a baking-dish just large enough to hold them all. Drizzle the honey over them then pour in the wine. Bake for 40 minutes, then test to see if they are ready by inserting a knife into each pear: it should just go through the centre. Eat hot or cold, but they are best served hot.

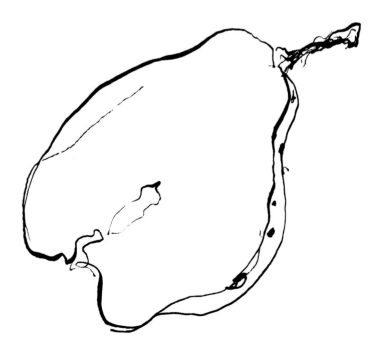

caramelised pear and parmesan tart

This tart, a relative of the apple, almond and stilton tart on page 78, will fill a savoury or sweet break in your day. I like to eat it with whipped cream as a pudding, but a thin slice is good as a snack on the run. Make sure you use freshly grated parmesan of the best quality. The next time you make it you may like to add extra cheese: in this recipe it's fairly subtle.

FOR 8 AS A DESSERT

caster sugar	*500 g*
water	*60 ml*
pears	*4, peeled, cored and quartered*
unsalted butter	*250 g, at room temperature*
parmesan	*100 g, finely grated*
breadcrumbs	*200 g, fresh*
eggs	*3, whisked together for 20 seconds*
sweet shortcrust tart shell	*1 x 30 cm, baked blind*

Pre-heat the oven to 180°c.

Place 300 g of the sugar and all of the water into a saucepan that will be large enough to hold the pears in a single layer. Bring it to the boil, stirring until the sugar has dissolved. Then cook on a rapid boil, without stirring, until it begins to darken, shaking the pan gently to make a uniform caramel. Once it turns a light caramel colour, carefully add the pears and stir gently, turning down the heat to medium. The pears will begin to release some of their juices into the caramel and the now thick mixture will slowly become a syrup. Cook until a skewer or sharp knife goes through the pears easily, then remove from the heat and leave to cool for 5 minutes.

Beat the remaining 200 g of sugar with the butter until light in colour. Mix in the parmesan, breadcrumbs and eggs, then stir in 30 ml of the pear syrup. Place this mixture in the tart shell – it should come two-thirds of the way up the side of the pastry. If some is left over bake it in another dish and eat it as a snack!

Drain the pears in a sieve or colander over a bowl, then sit them on top of the tart, pressing them in gently. Bake for 40 minutes. The tart is cooked when a thin knife inserted into the centre comes out moist but clean. Leave it to sit for at least an hour before eating, but it will keep in the fridge for up to 3 days. To serve as a dessert, drizzle some of the pear syrup over each portion.

CANAPÉS
& NIBBLES

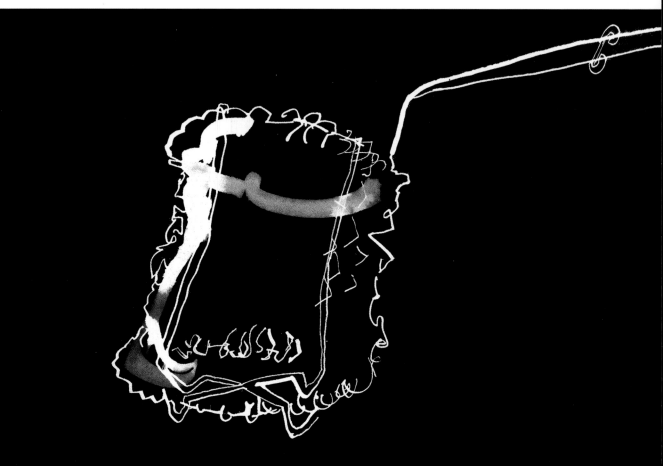

the reasons for
crostini

The main reason to make, and serve, crostini as a starter is that they are so simple, and you can make a huge assortment very quickly – you just need to assemble various topping ingredients: choose from chutneys, pestos, pastes and relishes, cheeses, roast vegetables, meats and fish of all descriptions, from cured to pickled or freshly grilled. Make your crostini a two-mouthful affair – any more and you're serving a sandwich!

All you need to do is slice some one- or two-day-old bread very thinly, brush it with a little olive oil, and cook it in a single layer on trays in a 180°c oven until golden and crisp. Leave to go cold, then either put on the topping and serve, or store in airtight containers for up to 1 week. Baguettes, ciabatta and soda bread are all good to use, but the main thing to keep in mind is that the slices shouldn't be so big that your guests can't hold them easily.

white bean and basil mash on crostini

This is really quick to make, but tastes as though it has taken you longer! You can cook your own beans from dried, of course, but I promise you, no one will know if you use canned. *For photograph see page 135*

FOR 15 CROSTINI

leeks	*100-150 g, trimmed, washed and finely sliced*
garlic	*1 clove, peeled and finely sliced*
extra-virgin olive oil	*20 ml*
cannellini beans	*420 g tin, drained and rinsed well*
salt	*1|2 teaspoon*
black pepper	*1|2 teaspoon, freshly ground*
large basil leaves	*8, finely shredded*

Sauté the leek and garlic in the oil until the leek turns golden, stirring occasionally. Add the beans, barely cover them with water, bring to the boil and put a lid on the pan. Cook for 5 minutes on a rapid simmer, then remove the lid, add the salt and pepper, and cook uncovered until all the water has evaporated. Take it off the heat and leave it to cool. Stir in the basil, and mash everything together with the back of a fork to produce a chunky paste. Spread it on crostini, drizzle with a little extra olive oil, and eat.

molly's vegemite toasts

Molly Gordon, my grandmother, was not a wasteful woman. She used to keep a jar of the most delicious snacks on the trolley in her kitchen. When I eventually asked her what they were, I was shocked! This is how you make them.

Pre-heat the oven to 120°c. Lightly, very lightly, butter any stale slices of bread you might have. Spread a thin layer of vegemite or marmite on top. Cut each slice into 4 fingers, taking the crusts off if you want to. Lay them on a lightly buttered baking-tray and bake for at least an hour, until they are crisp and golden. Leave to cool on a cake rack and store in airtight containers for up to 2 weeks.

spicy chicken and coconut soup in a cup

When we launched my first book, *The Sugar Club Cookbook*, at the restaurant in 1997, I wanted to serve a cross-section of all my favourite dishes. One such dish is laksa, to which I had dedicated a chapter. But how to serve it as a canapé? I realised that to offer small amounts I would have to dispense with the noodles or it would be too messy. This is what I devised.

For photograph see page 135

FOR 8 SMALLISH CUPS

small red onion	*1, peeled and finely diced*
hot red bird's-eye chilli	*1, finely sliced*
sesame oil	*20 ml*
garlic	*1 clove, peeled and finely sliced*
ginger	*1 thumb, finely julienned plus 1 thumbnail-sized piece, finely grated*
coconut milk	*400 ml*
chicken stock	*200 ml (although water will do at a squeeze)*
thai fish sauce	*2 teaspoons*
soy sauce	*1 teaspoon*
chicken breast	*1, skinned and boned*
coriander stems	*5, roughly chopped*
salt	*1/2 teaspoon*
spring onions	*2, finely sliced*
coriander leaves	*1/4 cup*

Sauté the onion and chilli in the sesame oil until coloured, then add the garlic and ginger julienne and fry over a high heat, stirring well, for 1 minute. Add the coconut milk and the chicken stock, bring to the boil, then simmer for 1 minute. Add the fish sauce and the soy sauce, and continue to cook on a low heat. Mince together the chicken, grated ginger, coriander stems and salt in a small food-processor (or chop it all as finely as you can) and roll the paste into 16 marble-sized balls. Turn up the broth to a gentle boil and drop in the dumplings. Put a lid on the pan and cook for 2 minutes. To serve, place 2 dumplings in each cup, pour on some broth and scatter over some spring onions and coriander leaves.

oyster fritters
with sour cream and chives

The oysters in these fritters, like any oyster you eat, have to be really fresh. Many people are scared of contracting food poisoning from eating shellfish, but when fresh, and handled properly by your fish supplier, it shouldn't present any problems. I like to serve a mound of them on a tray accompanied by fingers of buttered wholemeal toast and lemon wedges. I'd serve 2 oysters each as canapés.

FOR 6

eggs	*3, lightly beaten*
shallots	*2, peeled and finely sliced*
salt	*a pinch*
black pepper	*1/2 teaspoon, freshly ground*
oysters, and their shells	*12, washed and dried*
sour cream	*120 ml*
chives	*1/4 cup, finely sliced*
butter	*100 g*

Keep the oyster shells warm in the oven at 150°c while you're making the fritters.

Put the eggs, shallots, salt and pepper into a mixing bowl and whisk lightly. Add the oysters and stir to coat each one well. In a separate bowl mix the sour cream and chives. Heat a frying-pan and when it is hot add half of the butter. When it begins to brown, carefully spoon in one oyster at a time until the pan is comfortably full. Cook for 1 minute before carefully flipping over. Cook for only 15 seconds more, then remove the oysters from the pan and replace them in their shells. Serve while still warm with a dollop of the chive cream on top.

duck, ginger and peanut spring rolls
with ginger dipping sauce

I first made this dish in late 1997 for business and first-class passengers on Air New Zealand flights from London Heathrow to Los Angeles. They went down surprisingly well, so I've gone on to serve them at home and at the Sugar Club as canapés for various parties.

FOR 12-15 SPRING ROLLS

large duck legs	*2, approximately 500–600 g*
salt	*2 teaspoons*
ginger	*2 thumbs, peeled and finely minced*
roasted peanuts	*100 g, roughly chopped*
coriander leaves	*1 cup*
spring onions	*8, finely sliced*
spring-roll wrappers	*10–15 cm square*
egg	*1, beaten, to seal the wrappers*
soy sauce	*300 ml*
cider vinegar	*50 ml*
light honey	*50 ml*

Put the duck legs into a saucepan, cover them with cold water, add the salt, bring to the boil and simmer rapidly for 60 minutes. Remove from the heat and leave the meat to cool in the liquid. Remove and discard the skin, then take the flesh off the bones and shred it finely. Mix it with half of the ginger, all of the peanuts, the coriander and spring onions then taste for seasoning. Separate the spring-roll wrappers, then stack them on top of each other to prevent them drying out. (They separate best at room temperature.) Have them in front of you in the shape of a diamond. Brush the egg-wash along the corner furthest away from you, then place a heaped tablespoon or so of duck mixture, shaped into a fat sausage, running left to right in the centre. Roll the edge closest to you tightly over the filling, then fold each side (left and right) over it, overlapping slightly. Roll it away from you towards the egg-wash until you have a firm, sealed spring roll. Place it on a tray lined with clingfilm. Continue until you have used all the mixture.

Make the ginger dipping sauce: put the remaining ginger, the soy, vinegar and honey into a saucepan. Simmer to reduce by half, then strain.

Deep-fry the rolls in oil at 180°c, 6-8 at a time, until golden.

pork and duck rillettes

The first time I had really good rillettes was in Paris in 1986. I bought this rich fatty mixture from a deli, with some leeks vinaigrette and a baguette, and went and sat in the cemetery Père Lachaise, with a bottle of Burgundy and a glass to complete the meal. It was fantastically sunny and warm and I felt as if I was in a Jacques Tati movie. Rillettes are great to take on a picnic and good on a luncheon buffet, but I also like to serve them spread on crostini as a canapé. Make more than you need: they are a little time-consuming, and they'll keep, well covered, in the fridge for a month.

FOR 40 CROSTINI

large duck	*1, about 2 kg, breasts and legs removed, carcass discarded (use it for stock)*
pork belly	*1.5 kg, bones and rind removed*
garlic	*6 cloves*
cinnamon stick	*1/2*
bay leaves	*2*
lemon	*peel of 1*
coarse sea salt	*1 large teaspoon, plus extra*
black pepper	*1 teaspoon, freshly ground, plus extra*

Remove the bones from the duck legs. Cut the breast and leg meat roughly into 3cm dice. Cut the pork belly into 3cm dice. Place the meat and all the remaining ingredients into a heavy-bottomed pan and cover by 4cm with boiling water. Turn on the heat and bring to a rapid simmer, stirring well to ensure that the meat doesn't stick to the bottom. Place a lid on the pan and cook for 1 hour. Remove the lid and continue to cook until all the liquid has evaporated and the meat is almost frying in its natural fat. Take it off the heat and leave it to cool for 20 minutes, then remove the cinnamon, bay leaves and lemon. Using two forks, shred the meat – ideally you should be left with no large lumps. Taste for seasoning – you'll need to add about another 2 teaspoons of coarse sea salt. Pack the rillettes into clean jars or a terrine and press the mixture down firmly. Leave it to go cold, then cover it with a lid or clingfilm and leave it to sit for at least a day to allow the flavours to develop.

roast baby aubergines
with spiced yoghurt and mint

These make a tasty first course, an exciting canapé, or a great platter to add to a picnic. If you're unable to find baby aubergines, use the larger ones, cut into 1cm thick slices and cooked in the same way.

FOR 16 CANAPÉS

baby aubergines	*8*
garlic	*1 clove, peeled and finely chopped*
extra-virgin olive oil	*30 ml*
salt	
black pepper	*freshly ground*
cumin seeds	*1|2 teaspoon*
small red chilli	*1|4, finely chopped*
greek style yoghurt	*250 ml*

Pre-heat the oven to 200°c.

Cut the aubergines in half lengthways and score the flesh. Mix the garlic with half of the oil, some salt and pepper and brush it on the cut sides of the aubergines. Place them on a baking-tray lined with baking parchment and bake in the top third of the oven for 15-20 minutes, until a knife goes through the flesh easily. Leave them to cool before eating.

While the aubergines are cooking, heat the remaining oil and add the cumin and chilli. Fry until golden then remove from the heat and stir into the yoghurt. Spoon the yoghurt mixture on to the aubergines and serve with a crisp salad and some toasted flat bread (Turkish, Indian, pitta, whatever you fancy).

quail's eggs and bacon on pikelets

This will make up to 20 pikelets, but it is difficult to halve the mixture. The topping ingredients are enough for 10 canapés.

flour	*150 g*
baking powder	*1 level teaspoon*
salt	*1/2 teaspoon*
sugar	*1/2 teaspoon*
egg	*1*
milk	*150 ml*
butter	*20 g plus extra for frying*
chives	*2 tablespoons, finely sliced*
smoked streaky bacon	*5 rashers, rind removed*
cooking oil	*for frying the eggs*
quail's eggs	*10*
extra chives	*for garnishing*

Sift the first 4 ingredients into a bowl. Beat the egg and milk together. Make a well in the centre of the dry ingredients and gradually whisk in the milk, making sure there are no lumps. Heat the butter in a frying-pan until it goes nut brown, then whisk it into the pikelet mixture, and stir in the sliced chives. Put the pan back on to a moderate heat, add a little extra butter and drop in generous teaspoonfuls of the batter: ideally, the pikelets will be of a similar size to a cooked quail's egg. Once air bubbles form on top of the pikelets, turn them over and cook them for another minute, then remove from the heat. Once all the pikelets are done, it's time to cook the bacon. Either fry it in the pan you used to cook the pikelets, or grill, until slightly crispy. Cut each cooked rasher into 4 – again, the pieces should be about the same size as the cooked eggs. Lay the bacon pieces on the pikelets and keep warm. Wipe out the pan, heat it again and add a little oil. The best way to crack open a quail's egg is to lay it on a board and, using a sharp, pointed knife, cut downwards gently through the shell, avoiding the yolk. Pop the eggs into the pan and cook them until the white has just set but the yolks are still glossy and runny. Sit a cooked egg on top of the bacon, sprinkle with the chives and eat while hot.

COCKTAILS
CORDIALS
TEAS & COFFEES

when we eat, we also
drink,

...so I thought I'd give you some ideas for drinks that range from healthy and refreshing through to those that are downright alcoholic. I use the same theory for mixing flavours in drinks as I do in meals; the combinations I use may sometimes seem a little odd, but the flavours will work together, for whatever reasons.

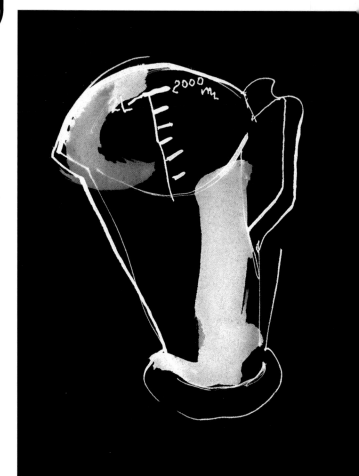

michael's fresh pineapple piña colada in a blender

We used to live in a beautiful rose-covered wooden house at Karaka Bay in Wellington, New Zealand, which looked over the harbour. Almost opposite the house was a jetty that ran out into the harbour, where a small pod of killer whales once swam underneath. This was also the jetty we dived off for our swims! This cocktail was a feature of any weekend brunch we gave. It's important that the pineapple is incredibly sweet, but if you can't find a good one, use an extra 300 ml of pineapple juice.

FOR 4 TALL 350 ML GLASSES

ice cubes	*enough to fill 2 glasses*
fresh pineapple	*300 g*
pineapple juice	*300 ml*
unsweetened coconut milk	*400 ml*
white rum	*100 ml*
caster sugar	*2 tablespoons (optional, taste the drink and decide)*

Blend everything together for 2 minutes, then pour it out, sit back and watch the sun go down.

freshly blended bloody mary

Everyone has their favourite recipe for a Bloody Mary, but I like mine made with slightly chunky sun-ripened fresh tomatoes.

FOR 4

tomatoes	*600 g, ripe, sweet, washed and quartered*
red chilli	*1/2, with the seeds, finely sliced*
horseradish	*1/2 teaspoon, freshly grated (or from the jar)*
vodka	*100 ml*
ripe limes	*juice of 2*
unrefined caster sugar	*2 teaspoons*
salt	*a pinch*
celery stalk	*1/2, finely sliced*
ice cubes	*2 cups*
cucumber	*1/4, seeds removed, cut into long batons*
black pepper	*freshly ground*

Place everything except the ice, cucumber and pepper in a blender. Purée for 10 seconds, scrape down the bowl and purée for a further 5 seconds. Add the ice and purée for 10 seconds more. Pour into tall glasses, place some cucumber in each one, and grind some pepper over the top.

vicki gordon's best ever fruity fizzy cocktail

My eldest sister Vicki, who lives in Sydney, is a great cocktail party hostess and this is one of her current favourites. It's important that you use only very ripe fruit in this or the flavour will be a little dull. Guavas are sometimes hard to get in Britain: if you can't find one replace it with ripe papaya or mango, or use guava juice.

FOR 4

strawberries	*12, hulled*
unrefined caster sugar	*1 teaspoon*
gin	*60 ml*
cointreau	*30 ml*
dry sparkling wine	*500 ml, chilled*
guava	*4–8 slices*
juicy lime	*1, quartered, each segment lightly crushed*

Place the strawberries and sugar in a bowl and mash them with the back of a fork, then stir in the gin and Cointreau. Divide this mixture between 4 glasses, then half fill each glass with sparkling wine. Add some guava slices and a lime quarter to each glass, then top it up with more sparkling wine.

vodka, mango, beetroot and ginger cocktail

Ideally you will need a juice extractor for this, but if you don't mind a few lumps, you can get away with puréeing it in a blender. Beetroot may seem an odd ingredient for a cocktail, but it has a subtle earthy sweetness when raw, that complements the mango in this drink.

FOR 4

ginger	*30 g, skin scrubbed*
medium beetroot	*1, around 150 g, raw and peeled*
very ripe and sweet mangoes	*2, large, peeled and stoned*
vodka	*100 ml*
ice cubes	
lime peel	*for garnish*

Using a juice extractor, juice the ginger, beetroot and mangoes, and pour over the vodka in a jug. Stir well. Put ice cubes into glasses, pour over the cocktail and top with a little lime peel.

lemon, garlic and ginger tonic,
to ward off winter colds

This is a drink that seems to be made predominantly by New Zealand chefs working in British kitchens. It must come from all our mothers back home: once anyone at work starts to feel fluey, there'll be a couple of pots of it brewing on the stove before you know it, everyone with their own version. It really does make you feel better, and the garlic isn't overpowering. *For photograph see page 151*

FOR 2 BIG MUGS

medium-sized lemon	*1, cut into 12 slices, skin and all*
garlic	*3 cloves, peeled and roughly chopped or crushed*
ginger	*1/2 thumb, peeled and thinly sliced*
honey	*200 ml*
water	*600 ml*

Put all of the ingredients into a saucepan and bring it to the boil, then turn to a simmer, cover with a lid and cook for 10 minutes. Either strain it as you pour it or, if you're feeling like it, eat the garlic and lemon from the mug – it's all good for you. Drink it while it's hot.

cardamom coffee

In our fridge we keep a jar of cardamom coffee that two good friends, Gianni and Adrian, brought back from Turkey. There are times when it seems the best drink in the world, especially after a spicy meal or late at night when you need the edge taken off the caffeine. However you make your coffee – espresso machine, drip filter, percolator (I'm talking real beans here not instant) – just add 1 cardamom pod, either ground with your beans or bashed flat with a rolling pin, to each person's coffee. The coffee is best drunk very strong and slightly sweet.

tamarind tea

I first had tamarind tea, the perfect thirst-quencher on a hot day, in Legian, Bali, in 1988, at a small café owned by a Balinese woman and a German man, which unfortunately no longer exists. Make a big potful (it's good hot or cold), leave it to cool and take it on a picnic in a Thermos flask with lots of ice. If you want to add a little sugar, do so when you pour on the boiling water. Wet tamarind comes in a sticky block, and can be bought at most Asian food stores, but you can use any available tamarind. The recipe couldn't be simpler.

FOR 4

wet tamarind *80 g*
boiling water *800 ml*

Place the tamarind in a teapot and pour on the water. Break up the tamarind a little with a spoon, then leave it to sit for 5 minutes. Stir well and strain into cups.

lemon-grass and ginger tea

The first time I remember encountering lemon-grass was when my cousin Rae brewed me some lemon-grass and lucerne tea as a healthy elixir to keep my energy up: I was then a young apprentice putting in far too many hours at work each week, up to a hundred over seven days. This tea revives your spirits, warms you in winter, or cools you in summer. Drink it hot, or leave it to cool and serve it over crushed ice.

FOR 4 LARGE CUPS

lemon grass *2 stems, bashed flat with a meat hammer or similar*
ginger *100 g, skin scrubbed, roughly chopped*
cold water *1 litre*
sugar *or elderflower cordial or honey to taste*

Put all of the above into a saucepan and bring it to the boil. Reduce the heat, put the lid on, and simmer for 5 minutes. Strain before drinking.

coffee granita

A simple classic, best served with lightly sweetened whipped cream and a crunchy plain biscuit.

FOR 4 AS A DESSERT

caster sugar	*150 g*
water	*200 ml*
strong black coffee	*600 ml, preferably espresso, chilled*

Place the sugar and water in a small pan and bring slowly to the boil, stirring until the sugar is dissolved. Once it reaches boiling point, stop stirring, and boil for 4 minutes. Take off the heat and leave to cool. Add the coffee, mix well, then pour into a shallow metal dish and place it in the freezer. Every 30 minutes stir it with a fork to break up the ice crystals. The granita should be ready within about 4 hours. Just before serving, mash it with a fork or a heavy whisk to break up any large ice crystals.

the best iced coffee

This is my favourite iced coffee, made quick, thick and frothy. If you don't have a blender, shake it up in a jar!

FOR 2

very strong espresso	*200 ml (equivalent to 4 regular espressos)*
unrefined caster sugar	*2 teaspoons*
large ice cubes	*12*
cold milk	*100 ml*

Put everything in a blender and blend on high for 15 seconds. What could be simpler?

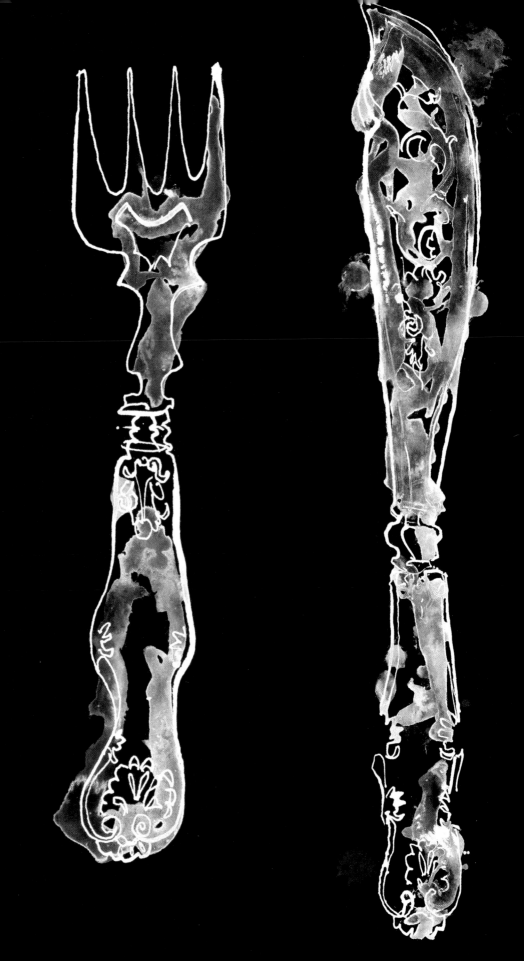

DINNER
PARTIES

THE MENUS

I don't get to
cook at home

too often but when I do, I pull out all the stops. It's a great way to catch up with a lot of friends at once, and it makes a great change from the slog of the restaurant. Usually when people arrive, I'll still be in the kitchen, but I like them to come and chat as I finish up, maybe get them to help me as I plod along with a drink beside me. The following are some of the dinner parties I've cooked over the last year.

michael's birthday

for 8

Michael McGrath, my partner, celebrates his birthday on 1 January. This has to be the worst day of the year (with the possible exception of Christmas Day) for a celebration of this kind. Most people have other things on their minds, such as how best to recover from welcoming in the new year – or, more pressingly, what on earth to do with it now it's arrived. So, Michael's birthday dinner is usually a luxurious feast of many flavours and textures to make up for the fact that people tend to forget it. He enjoys healthy food with fresh, well-defined flavours – hence his fondness for Japanese cuisine. This is what I cooked for him on 1 January 1999. We drank vodka martinis, followed by champagne and Pinot Noir. There was more champagne with the cake, then herbal tea or strong coffee to end.

roast pumpkin
with cashew-nut and gomasio dressing

Gomasio dates back to when Michael was macrobiotic, in 1982, when he was living in Sydney. It's traditionally made by grinding with a pestle in a ridged mortar called a suribachi, but a regular mortar and pestle will do. The most important ingredient in this relatively simple dish is the pumpkin, so make sure you hunt out the sweetest and tastiest there is.

For photograph see page 159

pumpkin	*1.5 kg – or butternut squash – skin on and seeds removed*
salt	
black pepper	*freshly ground*
sesame oil	*30 ml*
toasted sesame seeds	*50 g*
sea salt	*20 g*
cashew nuts	*120 g, toasted until golden, then finely chopped*
mirin	*100 ml*
lemon juice	*100 ml*
rocket	*a large bunch*

Pre-heat the oven to 180°c. Cut the pumpkin into 8 even-sized chunks and place them in an ovenproof dish. Lightly season with salt and pepper, drizzle over the sesame oil, then pour in 400 ml boiling water. Roast in the top part of the oven until cooked, around 40-80 minutes, depending on the type of pumpkin you use. Test to see if it's cooked by inserting a sharp knife into the centre, much as you would a potato. While it's cooking, make the dressing: grind the lightly toasted sesame seeds and salt together with a pestle in a mortar or in a spice grinder. When you have a fine powder, tip it into a bowl with the cashew nuts, mirin and lemon juice. Mix well and leave to sit until the pumpkin is cooked. Place one piece of the hot pumpkin on a plate and scatter some rocket on top of it. Check the dressing for seasoning and adjust if necessary, then pour it over the rocket.

soy, star anise and ginger-baked salmon
with soba noodle, seaweed and cucumber salads

Salmon is one of Michael's favourite fish, and it lends itself well to these flavoured salads. It's the fattiness that does it, and mackerel or tuna will work just as well. Dried seaweed is readily available from health-food stores all over the country – I bought some 'mixed sea vegetables' recently in Chester, and I've seen hijiki, arame and wakame on sale in Edinburgh, so don't write to tell me it can't be purchased outside of London! Most seaweeds just need soaking before you eat them. Soba noodles are made from buckwheat and wheat flours and are widely available in supermarkets and delicatessens. *For photograph see page 163*

fresh ginger	*2 thumbs, finely julienned*
whole star anise	*8*
light soy sauce	*100 ml*
palm sugar	*1 teaspoon (demerara sugar would suffice)*
sesame oil	*50 ml*
salmon fillet	*1.6 kg, with skin, bones removed, cut into 8 equal pieces*
dried seaweed	*20 g – either arame, hijiki, fine wakame or mixed sea salad*
coriander	*1 bunch, leaves only*
large cucumber	*1, peeled, seeded and julienned*
lemon juice	*100 ml*
caster sugar	*2 teaspoons*
dried soba noodles	*300 g*
sesame oil	*20 ml, plus a little extra*
spring onions	*5, finely sliced*

Mix together the first 5 ingredients and pour over the salmon. Leave it to marinate for 2 hours, turning it twice during that time.

Meanwhile, make the salads. Place the seaweed in a heatproof bowl and pour on enough hot water to cover. Leave for 30 minutes, then drain it and mix it with the coriander. Place the cucumber in a bowl with the lemon juice and sugar. Stir it, then cover and put to one side. Bring 2 litres of water to the boil in a deep saucepan. Add the noodles and stir gently after 30 seconds. Bring back to the boil and add 1 big coffee cup of cold water to the pan. Again bring it to the boil, and add another cup of cold water. When it comes to the boil again, test a noodle: it should be *al dente* (but if not cook a little longer). Drain the noodles in a colander and gently run cold water over them, tossing carefully. When they are cold toss them with the remaining sesame oil and the spring onions.

When the fish is ready to cook, heat the oven to 230°c and place a ceramic heatproof dish in the oven to warm through. Brush the dish with a little sesame oil then put in the salmon, skin side up, and pour the marinade over it. Place it in the top third of the oven and cook for just 8 minutes – salmon is best served medium to rare. Remove it from the oven and leave it to sit for a few minutes before you eat it.

Mix together the seaweed and soba noodles and divide the salad on to 8 plates. Sit a piece of salmon on it and drizzle over some of the cooking juices. Pile the cucumber on top and pour over some of the cucumber juice.

goat's cheese with spiced roasted pear

Goat's cheese is the most popular cheese in our fridge at home and some fantastic British and Irish varieties are available in supermarkets as well as in fine cheese shops. Buy whatever is ripe and ready. An hour before you serve the pumpkin starter, take the cheese from the fridge to let it mature. You can cook the pears in advance if you need to save time – they will keep for up to 5 days in the fridge. *For photographs see page 158*

mild red chilli	*1, green stem removed, finely chopped*
lemon grass	*1 stem, outside 3 layers discarded, finely sliced*
cinnamon stick	*4cm piece, broken up*
allspice	*1/2 teaspoon, finely ground*
cider vinegar	*30 ml*
demerara sugar	*120 g*
water	*150 ml*
large sweet (but firm) pears	*4, cored and cut in half lengthways*
goat's cheese	*400 g*

Pre-heat the oven to 180°c. Mix together the first 6 ingredients in a bowl, then stir in the water. Place the pears in a small ovenproof dish, just large enough to hold them. Pour the chilli mixture over them and cook for 1 hour, when a sharp knife should go through the flesh easily. Leave them to cool to room temperature.

To serve, place a nice chunk of cheese on each plate with a pear alongside it. Drizzle some of the cooking syrup over both the pear and the cheese, then eat.

warm walnut whiskey and sultana cake
with mango and mascarpone – and candles, of course

One cold 1 January, in London, I reheated this cake on a griddle to serve as a pudding, but it works well on a tea trolley on a sunny afternoon – or, indeed, as a wedding cake, covered with marzipan. The mango and mascarpone add that Asian-fusion touch I love so much!

Any left overs will keep in an airtight tin for 3 days in a cool place.

FOR 10-12

walnut halves	*200 g*
sultanas	*250 g or raisins, currants, muscatels or a mixture*
butter	*280 g, at room temperature, cut into 2cm chunks*
light brown sugar	*400 g*
eggs	*3*
Irish whiskey	*120 ml*
flour	*350 g*
baking powder	*3 teaspoons*
large ripe mangoes	*2, stoned, peeled and cut into chunks*
mascarpone	*200 g*

Pre-heat the oven to 160°c. Line a 30cm cake tin with non-stick baking parchment. Put the walnuts and sultanas in a saucepan and cover them with cold water. Bring it to the boil, then simmer rapidly for 10 minutes. Drain them in a colander, discarding the liquid, and return them to the pan. Add the butter to the pan and stir over a low heat until it has melted. In a large bowl, beat together the eggs and sugar for 30 seconds, then stir in the walnut mixture and the whiskey. Sift the flour and baking powder into the mixture and stir to incorporate. Spoon the cake mixture into the tin and bake it in the centre of the oven for 40-50 minutes. The cake is cooked when a thin knife or skewer inserted in the centre comes out clean. Leave the cake to cool in the tin. Turn out. Spread the mascarpone over it and scatter on the mango, then add a few candles – and happy birthday, Michael.

asian
feast for 4

Many of the flavours, aromas and textures of Asia collide in this menu. It's South-east Asian inspired (think Indonesia, Malaysia, Thailand and Burma), with no specific roots! Serve the prawns and the pork at the same time, then follow it up with the stir-fry (with or without rice), and finally the rather tacky-looking, but delicious, dessert. I'd serve fruit cocktails to start, and either beer or a Riesling throughout.

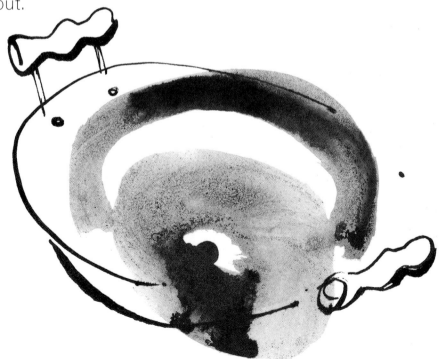

ginger-marinated pork salad
with green tea noodles, shiitake mushrooms and sesame

Green tea noodles are literally that: wheat noodles made with the addition of powdered Japanese green tea. You can often find them at health-food shops, but if you can't, substitute any other Asian noodle. Shiitake mushrooms are easy to find in supermarkets, but any good firm mushroom will work OK. *For photograph see page 167*

pork loin	*400 g, trimmed of all sinew*
ginger	*1 thumb, finely grated*
	plus 1/2 thumb, peeled and finely julienned
sea salt	*1/2 teaspoon*
caster sugar	*1/2 teaspoon*
sesame oil	*2 teaspoons*
sesame seeds	*2 teaspoons*
shiitake mushrooms	*8, stems discarded, finely sliced*
light soy sauce	*100 ml*
mirin	*100 ml*
green tea noodles	*120 g*
salad oil	*10 ml*
cooking oil	*1 tablespoon*

Mix the grated ginger, salt, sugar, oil and sesame seeds into a paste. Rub it into the pork and refrigerate for 2 hours. Place the shiitake in a small pan with the soy, mirin and julienned ginger, cover it and bring it to the boil, then uncover and simmer for 2 minutes. Turn off the heat and leave to cool. Cook the noodles in plenty of salted water until *al dente*, drain and refresh them in cold water. Drain well, then toss with the salad oil to prevent them sticking to each other. Pre-heat the oven to 200°c. Heat an ovenproof pan on the stove, then pour into it the cooking oil, add the pork, and cook over a moderate heat, turning to brown it on all sides. Place the pan in the oven and cook until the meat is just done, about 8-12 minutes depending on the thickness of the meat. Remove from the oven and leave to cool.

To serve, slice the pork thinly and divide it among the 4 plates. Pile the noodles on top, then spoon over the mushrooms and their cooking liquor.

prawn and ginger sleeping-bags
with green mango and coriander salad

When I started to make these I thought I'd call them wontons, but when they were all rolled up, they actually looked like the Prawn Scout Group asleep in their sleeping-bags. Anyway…the wonton wrappers make a good textural contrast to the sweetness of the plump flesh, especially when the prawns are mixed with the ginger. If you can't get wonton wrappers, you could either fry the prawns in batter or crumb them.

A green mango is not an unripe mango, but one that is only ever eaten green, when it is crunchy and tart. You'll have to buy it from a Thai food store. A good substitute would be a mixture of finely julienned sour apple and carrot.

green mango	*1*
large shallots	*2, peeled and finely sliced*
thai fish sauce	*1 teaspoon*
lime juice	*40 ml*
caster sugar	*1 tablespoon*
coriander leaves	*1 cup*
raw prawns	*16, heads removed*
fresh ginger	*1 teaspoon, finely grated*
wonton wrappers	*16 x 6–8cm square*
small coriander stems	*16 – just use the tips*
egg	*1, beaten, for egg wash*
oil	*for deep-frying*

Peel the mango, remove the two lobes of flesh from the stone, then finely julienne the flesh. Put it in a bowl with the shallots, fish sauce, lime juice and caster sugar, stir well then scatter the coriander leaves on top. Peel the shell from the prawns, but keep the tail intact, then mix the prawns with the ginger. Lay the wonton wrappers on a worktop, 4 at a time, and put a prawn in the centre of each and place a coriander stem alongside it. Brush one side of the wrappers with egg-wash, then fold the unbrushed side over the prawn and gently, but tightly, roll them up. Repeat until all the prawns are in their 'sleeping-bags'. Heat at least 5cm of oil in a wok, saucepan or deep-fryer. When it reaches 180°c, the usual temperature for deep-frying, add the prawns. Cook only as many at a time as will comfortably fit into the pan. Fry for 1 minute, then turn them over and cook for a further 30 seconds. Don't overcook them or they'll become dry and tough. Remove from the pan and drain on absorbent paper. Repeat until all the prawns are cooked. Mix the coriander into the mango salad and serve with the prawns.

fiery chicken, green chilli and lemon-grass stir-fry
with rice noodles, peanuts, coconut and bok choy

dried rice noodles	*100 g*
bok choy	*8*
chicken breasts	*4, skinned and boned*
garlic	*4 cloves, peeled and finely sliced*
hot green chillies	*2–4, finely sliced, with seeds*
lemon grass	*4 stems, the outer 3 layers removed, the inside finely sliced (discard the dry upper and lower ends)*
peanut oil	*50 ml*
sugar	*2 teaspoons*
thai fish sauce	*20 ml*
coconut milk	*500 ml, unsweetened*
mint leaves	*1/2 cup*
coriander leaves	*1/2 cup*
spring onions	*2, finely sliced*
toasted peanuts	*100 g, roughly chopped*
lime juice	*20 ml*
salt	

I remember when the wok seemed exotic – until chefs like Ken Hom suddenly made it seem an essential implement in the kitchen. . . so I'm going to assume you have a wok with a lid, and gas jets. If you don't, this dish will be a little harder to make in a frying-pan on an electric hotplate, but the end result will be fine. Having said that, I was in London's Chinatown recently and bought 4 woks for £4.50 each – almost nothing for a piece of equipment that can last a lifetime.

Rice noodles come in myriad shapes and sizes, long and thin, wide and flat. The very fine ones don't take much soaking, but the fatter, wide ones may be best left to soak in warm water at the back of the stove for an hour – just keep your eye on them.

Pour enough boiling water on the noodles to cover them and leave them for 20-60 minutes (see introduction). Cut the bok choy in half lengthways and wash it gently in cold water, then drain. Slice the chicken into strips 1/2cm thick and mix it with the garlic, half of the chillies, a third of the lemon grass and half of the peanut oil. Leave everything until the noodles are firm but almost pliable, then proceed. Place the wok over the fiercest heat until it is smoking, then add the oil and swirl it around. Immediately throw in the remaining chillies and stir quickly, then add the chicken mixture and the sugar, stir well and fry for 20 seconds. Add the remaining lemon grass, mix well, then pour in the fish sauce. Drain the noodles and add them to the wok, laying them flat on top. Cover them with the bok choy, then pour over the coconut milk. Put a lid on the wok and cook on high for 3-4 minutes, by which time everything will be ready. Mix the herbs with the spring onion and put them to one side. Stir the peanuts and lime juice into the wok. Taste for seasoning and add some salt if needed. Spoon the contents of the wok into 4 bowls and sprinkle the herbs on top.

cendol bur bur cha cha (it tastes great!)

This strange dessert takes its name from two of the many varieties of sweet iced desserts found throughout South-east Asia, so forgive its name and just make it. The addition of food colouring makes it look quite gaudy, but think of it being served from a street food-stall in Java surrounded by water buffaloes, wagonloads of jackfruit, the sweet smell of Asia and lots of sun, and suddenly the colours will seem more at home. You can prepare all of the components up to 12 hours in advance, and assemble it when you want to eat it.

cornflour	*100 g*
cold water	*450 ml*
caster sugar	*60 g plus 100 g*
red food colouring	*1/2 teaspoon*
tapioca	*100 g*
water	*1 litre*
green food colouring	*1/2 teaspoon*
orange sweet potato	*250 g, peeled and cut into 1cm dice*
demerara sugar	*100 g*
ice cubes	*8*
palm sugar	*150 g, crumbled or grated*
coconut milk	*500 ml*

First, make the 'noodles' by mixing together the first 4 ingredients in a saucepan and stirring well. Place the pan over a moderate heat and cook for 2-3 minutes, stirring constantly, until the mixture becomes very thick and translucent. Put the paste into a potato ricer or a small-nozzled piping bag, and force it into a bowl of iced water, which will set the noodles. Leave them to go cold, then store in a little water until needed. Place the tapioca, the 100 g of caster sugar, the water and the green food colouring in a small saucepan and slowly bring it to the boil, stirring gently. Simmer for just a few minutes until the tapioca is still a little *al dente*. Pour it through a strainer then gently rinse it in cold water, to prevent the grains sticking together in one large lump. Boil the sweet potato with the demerara sugar and just enough water to cover it until it is just cooked. Drain it and leave it to cool.

To assemble, divide the noodles, tapioca, sweet potato and ice among 4 glasses, sprinkle the palm sugar on top, then pour on the coconut milk. Give it a good stir before you eat it, and think of those water buffaloes.

warm weather
vege feast for 6

In warm weather, vegetables are sometimes all I want to eat – both meat and fish seem too heavy. I like to have a few dishes, all quite different in texture and colour, to form a little banquet, and the following is a good example. Served with bread, a green salad, interesting dressings and relishes, maybe some cheese and nuts, it's all you need.

cous cous, tomato, asparagus, pinenut and basil salad

We usually eat cous cous hot, with spicy meals, as the Moroccans do, but it also makes a delicious salad as it absorbs dressings well. This one smells of summer, and the chewy cous cous makes a great contrast with the crisp vegetables.

instant cous cous	*400 g*
tepid water	*500 ml*
salt	*1 teaspoon*
black pepper	*1/2 teaspoon, freshly ground*
pinenuts	*100 g*
extra-virgin olive oil	*80 ml*
asparagus spears	*15*
cherry tomatoes	*24, cut in half, or 9 plum tomatoes, quartered*
basil leaves	*12–15, torn into 'chunks'*

Place the cous cous in a bowl and pour on the water, then stir in the salt and pepper. Place the pinenuts and olive oil in a small pan and fry them over a moderate heat until the nuts are golden, then tip them and the oil immediately on to the cous cous and mix well. Bring a pot of salted water to the boil and add the asparagus. Bring it back to the boil and cook for 1 minute. Drain and refresh the asparagus in cold water, then cut it into 3cm lengths. To finish the salad, add the asparagus, tomato and basil to the cous cous and toss everything together.

carrot, caraway, cumin, dill
and sweet potato fritters with yoghurt

I like to serve these fritters on a large platter and let people help themselves, but they're also good if you lay them on a plate, pile a simple green salad on top and serve them as a first course. Whatever you do, they make a good colourful addition to a meal. Orange sweet potatoes are becoming easier to find, these days, but you could substitute white ones, or even regular baking potatoes.

medium carrots	*2, around 300 g, peeled and tops removed*
orange sweet potatoes	*500 g, peeled*
medium red onion	*1, peeled*
egg	*1, lightly beaten*
cornflour	*60 g*
caraway seeds	*1 teaspoon, dry toasted until golden*
cumin seeds	*1 teaspoon, dry toasted until golden*
dill	*1 small bunch, roughly chopped*
salt	*1 teaspoon*
black pepper	*1/2 teaspoon, freshly ground*
oil	*for cooking*
thick, greek-style yoghurt	*200 ml*

Pre-heat the oven to 180°c. Grate the carrots, potatoes and the onion on a coarse grater, or on the grater attachment of a food-processor. Using your hands, squeeze out as much liquid as possible, then sit the mixture in a colander or large sieve and leave it to drain for 5 minutes. Place the egg, the cornflour, the seeds, the dill and the salt and pepper in a large bowl and mix well, then stir in the potato mixture. Divide the mixture into 6 balls, then press them to about 1 cm thick. Heat a frying-pan and pour in oil to a depth of about 3 mm. Place as many fritters as will comfortably fit into the pan, don't overcrowd them, and fry over a moderate heat until golden. Carefully flip each one over – they occasionally stick to the pan, then break apart as you try to turn them – and cook on the other side until golden. Repeat with the remaining fritters. Then place them on a lightly greased baking-tray and put them in the oven for 10-15 minutes, until they are cooked through. Serve either hot or cold, with a dollop of yoghurt on top.

braised red chicory and olives with macadamia nuts

Although this dish is lovely eaten cold in summer, it also works well as a side dish in winter alongside risotto, a simple pasta or roast vegetables (or meat!). Macadamia nuts are a personal favourite, but any well-toasted nut will be fine, and green chicory will happily replace the red variety. I have served this in the restaurant as a starter with buffalo mozzarella but without the nuts, and it went down a storm.

large red chicory	*6*
extra-virgin olive oil	*60 ml*
thyme	*1 very small bunch*
garlic	*2 cloves, finely sliced*
olives	*24–30, choose your favourite variety*
red wine	*250 ml*
balsamic vinegar	*30 ml*
parsley	*1/2 cup, chopped*
macadamia nuts	*100 g, lightly toasted and roughly chopped*

Preheat the oven to 180°c.

Slice the chicory in half lengthways and remove any discoloured leaves. Heat the oil in a frying-pan and lay the chicory in it, cut side down, and cook over a moderate heat until golden. Add the thyme, garlic and olives, and continue to cook until the garlic begins to go golden. Transfer the contents of the pan to an oven-proof dish, then pour the wine and vinegar into the frying-pan. Bring it to the boil and pour it over the chicory, then season lightly with salt and freshly ground black pepper. Cover the dish tightly with foil and bake for 40 minutes. Take it out of the oven, remove the foil and leave to cool. Just before serving, scatter the parsley and the nuts over the top.

grilled pineapple and mango
with tamarind and maple sauce

This is fairly straightforward to prepare, and the sauce can be made a day in advance. Tamarind paste can be found in almost any Asian supermarket, and is also appearing in supermarkets, although be wary of using any variety that tastes as if it contains vinegar, which will ruin the fruit: if in doubt, it's better not to use it, and add 20 ml extra lime or lemon juice instead.

mangoes	*3*
medium pineapple	*1*
tamarind paste	*50 ml*
maple syrup	*140 ml*
lime juice	*20 ml*
cinnamon	*1/2 teaspoon, freshly ground*
nutmeg	*a good pinch, freshly grated*

Turn your grill full on. Peel the mangoes, cut the 2 lobes of flesh from each stone, then lay these flat on a board and cut them in half horizontally. Top and tail the pineapple, cut off the skin and quarter it lengthways. Cut out the core, and slice each segment into 4. Lightly oil a foil-lined tray and lay the mango and pineapple on it in a single layer. Place it under the grill, as close to the heat as you can get it, and cook until the natural sugars in the fruit begin to caramelise. Turn the fruit over and cook again until it colours. (You can also do this on a char-grill or barbecue.) While the fruit is cooking, make the sauce. Place all the remaining ingredients in a saucepan. Bring it to the boil, stirring to dissolve the tamarind paste, then take it off the heat. Divide the fruit among 6 plates and serve with the sauce. This is great eaten with thick cream or ice cream.

fish feast for 4

I adore fish, and I love the endless ways it can be prepared, preserved and cooked. The following recipes give a really good cross-section of ways to handle different fish. There's no particular order in which you should serve the dishes – we just plonked it all down at once and let people help themselves as they thought fit. Bread is a must with this dinner, and so is a well-chilled beer or champagne. As for dessert, in New Zealand you can get fish-shaped chocolate-coated marshmallows called – surprisingly – 'Chocolate Fish', but that probably isn't of much help to you. After a meal like this, just serve fresh fruit.

marinated sour salad of sea bass, lemon grass and roast coconut

I like to make this dish with sea bass as it has a sweet, flaky, firm flesh that is particularly enhanced by the dressing. You could also use other firm white fish, such as turbot, snapper, bream or cod. It may seem excessive to crack open a whole coconut for a garnish, but the end result is well worth it.

sea bass fillet	*400 g, scales and bones removed, cut on an angle into 1/3–1/2cm slices*
lemon juice	*50 ml*
thai fish sauce	*10 ml*
tamarind paste	*20 ml*
garlic	*1 clove, peeled and finely sliced*
lemon grass	*1 stem, outer 3 layers and bottom 2cm discarded, finely sliced*
coconut	*1 (long-thread or ribbon coconut would also work)*
salad oil	*20 ml*
spring onions	*2, finely sliced*

Pre-heat the oven to 160°c. Mix together the lemon juice, fish sauce, tamarind paste, garlic and lemon grass in a bowl, then put in the sea bass and toss gently. Place the bowl in the fridge for 1 hour. Deal with the coconut outside: it's safer to hit it on the ground than risk bashing a hole in your kitchen floor if you miss. Wrap it in a tea-towel and tap it rather heavily with a hammer or the back of a knife until it cracks, turning it a bit each time. Strain the coconut milk into a glass and drink it – it's delicious and refreshing. Prise away the flesh from the shell (an oyster knife or screw-driver is good for this). Use a potato peeler to shave ribbons from the nut and toss them with the oil. Lay on a baking-sheet and roast until golden, tossing gently to ensure even cooking, for about 10-15 minutes.

Stir the spring onions into the fish mixture, then divide the salad on to 4 plates and sit the toasted coconut on top.

mussels and clams steamed with lime leaf, cucumber and baby corn

This is a fun, hands-on dish – there's no other way to eat it, really. Serve it with finger-bowls and paper napkins. Buy only the freshest shellfish, and discard any with broken shells. Remove the 'beards' from the mussels, and any barnacles. Wash all the shellfish well in lots of cold water, discard any that float and any that remain open once washed. Allow 600 g of shellfish per person if you plan to serve this on its own with salad and bread, but if there are to be a number of other dishes, 250 g mussels and 150 g clams per person will be plenty – with lots of bread to mop up the juices.

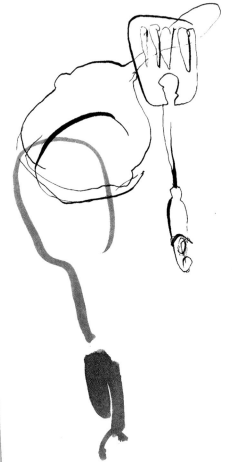

medium red onion	*1, peeled and finely sliced*
light cooking oil	*50 ml*
baby corn	*12*
lime leaves	*8*
mussels	*1 kg, prepared as above*
clams	*600 g, prepared as above*
medium cucumber	*1, unpeeled, finely sliced at an angle*
fish stock	*200 ml or dry white wine*

In a large saucepan, fry the onion in the oil until it is just beginning to colour, then add the baby corn and the lime leaves and fry over a moderate heat for 1 minute, stirring twice. Remove half of the mixture and put it in a bowl. Add half of the mussels, half of the clams and half of the cucumber to the saucepan and mix well. Put the baby-corn mixture back in the pan with the remaining shellfish and cucumber, then stir briefly. Pour in the wine, put a lid on and cook over a high heat for 2 minutes. Stir well then continue to cook, with the lid on, for another minute. By now all the shellfish should have opened, but if not keep the pot on a high boil until most have. Discard any that remain firmly closed, then take the saucepan to the table with a big ladle, serve and eat.

mackerel marinated in sweet soy,
on grilled aubergine, sesame and garlic purée with radish

The Japanese make a delicious dish by grilling lightly marinated eel fillet over an hibachi brazier, which inspired me to produce this one with one of my favourite fish, the much underrated mackerel.

soy sauce	*100 ml*
demerara sugar	*30 g*
ground star anise	*1 teaspoon*
ginger	*1 thumb, finely sliced*
cinnamon	*1 teaspoon, powdered*
medium mackerel fillets	*4, with skin on but bones removed*
large aubergine	*1, sliced lengthways into 4*
sesame oil	*30 ml*
garlic	*2 cloves, peeled and finely chopped*
sesame seeds	*3 teaspoons*
radishes	*6, finely sliced*

Place the first 5 ingredients in a small saucepan and bring it to the boil, then turn down the heat to a simmer and reduce by half. Strain the liquid into a bowl and leave it to cool. Then put in the mackerel and leave it to marinate for 5 minutes on each side.

Meanwhile, brush the aubergine with the sesame oil. Lay the slices on a lightly oiled baking-tray and grill them until they are brown. Turn them over and grill until they are golden. Then sprinkle them with the garlic and sesame seeds and grill again until the garlic begins to brown. Remove them from the heat and leave to cool, then purée in a food-processor until smooth. Check the seasoning and add some salt. Drain the soy marinade from the mackerel and lay the fish on the oiled baking-tray. Cook under a high heat, skin side down, until the flesh is golden, then turn and cook for around 2 minutes. Don't let them burn. Remove from the baking-tray and cut each fillet into 2. To serve, spoon some of the purée on to a plate, sit 2 pieces of mackerel on top, then scatter over the radish slices.

crab, mango and coriander omelette rolls

This recipe is inspired by a Danish chef who once worked with us at the Sugar Club in London. Carsten Pedersen brought great enthusiasm into the kitchen, for everything except working on Sundays. These days, he's cooking up a great storm back in Copenhagen (and now he *has* to work on Sundays!).

eggs	*2*
spring onions	*3, finely sliced*
thai fish sauce	*1 teaspoon, or a good pinch of salt and an extra teaspoon of water*
cold water	*2 dessertspoons*
light cooking oil	
large mango	*1, very ripe*
coriander	*12 stems, washed, leaves removed*
crab meat	*200 g, broken into chunks (crayfish or lobster also works well)*

In a bowl, whisk the eggs lightly, then mix in the spring onions, fish sauce and water until well combined. Heat a 20 cm frying-pan – non-stick is the best – and add a few drops of light cooking oil. Turn the heat to medium. When the pan is hot, pour in a quarter of the egg mixture and swirl it around to make a thin 'crêpe'. Leave it on the heat until the top looks set, then gently flip it over for 5 seconds and then slide the omelette out of the pan. Make another 3 omelettes.

Peel the mango, cut the flesh away from the stone with a sharp knife and slice it finely.

Lay an omelette flat and place a quarter of the mango and a quarter of the coriander on top. Place a quarter of the crab along the middle, then roll it up reasonably tightly. Repeat with the other omelettes. You can make the omelettes up to 6 hours ahead and roll them up an hour before you want to eat them.

left
overs

I love a good dinner, but I especially like looking in the fridge the next day, or the day after, and trying to come up with ideas of how best to utilise what's left over. Two very basic 'recipes' follow, then a list of ideas hopefully to inspire you! The very nature of left overs makes it almost impossible to give quantities of anything.

fried christmas cake with ice cream

My stepmother Rose would get us to finish the large, fruity, traditional Christmas cake her mother Nell had made for us every Christmas by disguising it in this dessert. I loved Nell's fruit cake, but you can eat only so much of it during a hot New Zealand summer. There is something rather moreish about this way of dealing with a Christmas cake – I guess it's the way the dried fruit caramelises when it's fried. All you need do is fry slices of cake, 1-2cm thick, in plenty of unsalted butter on a moderate heat for a few minutes on each side. Put a piece of cake on each plate, then scoop some ice cream on top.

roast meat (or salmon) and potato hash

A roast, or even a lovely poached *pot au feu*, will inevitably leave you with some odds and sods that may well sit in the fridge. I hate to see them wasted, so I recycle them for lunch or supper the next day. Two roast spuds, 200g left-over meat or poached salmon and an onion from the vegetable rack will make a great lunch for two.

Peel and slice the onion, then fry it in 100g butter or 50ml oil until it begins to caramelise. Add the spud and meat or fish, which you've cut roughly into 1cm dice and fry gently for 4 minutes, squashing it a bit with the back of a spoon. Let it catch on the bottom of the pan, so that there will be crunchy bits as well as moist smooth bits. At this point, if you have any left-over green vegetables, herbs or salad roughly chop them and mix them in. Eat on buttered toast.

ideas for left overs
chicken

Shred and toss with mayonnaise, chopped tomatoes, basil and iceberg lettuce for sandwiches.
Dice, then gently warm with double cream, English mustard and sliced mushrooms. Eat on toast, or in a vol-au-vent.
Dice finely and add to miso soup, with some noodles and tofu, for a quick supper dish.
Slice and mix with left-over potatoes and vegetables, season generously then mix in a few eggs. Pour into a tart shell and bake until golden.

pork

Slice finely and fry in a wok in peanut or sesame oil with plenty of minced garlic and ginger. Add mange tout or bok choy, grated carrots, toasted peanuts and soy sauce, then serve with rice.
Mince, or process in a food-processor, then mix with a beaten egg and some fresh breadcrumbs. Roll into patties and fry gently. Serve with apple sauce.

lamb

Fry some onions and cumin seeds in olive oil until golden, add finely sliced lamb, chopped fresh mint, fresh tomatoes and left-over cooked rice or new potatoes. Cover with a lid and bake for 10 minutes at 180°c.

Mince finely, add some mashed sweet potato and chopped coriander. Shape into rissoles, dust with flour, bake until golden and serve with mint sauce.

beef

Slice thinly and mix with horseradish cream, grated raw or cooked beetroot and chopped hard-boiled eggs. Eat in a sandwich or as bruschetta.

Fry chopped red onion and garlic in butter until golden, add chopped left-over cabbage and chopped roast beef. Fry on a high heat and season with Thai fish sauce and toasted cashew nuts.

fish

Flake and mix with mashed potato and fresh herbs. Form the mixture into cakes, then dust with flour, roll in egg-wash and breadcrumbs. Fry in olive oil or butter, and eat with capers and mayonnaise.

Flake the fish and mix with sliced cooked potatoes, a little cream and a few eggs. Add chopped fresh herbs, pour into a tart shell and bake until golden.

Flake the fish and mix it into cold soba noodles with lots of chopped fresh coriander, red chillies, spring onions and chives. Drizzle with soy sauce and sesame oil

vegetables

Place in a blender with vegetable stock and purée well. Warm the soup gently in a pan with either a little cream or yoghurt, but don't boil. Serve with crisp croûtons.

Roughly chop, then add to a plain risotto just at the end with a lot of freshly grated parmesan or good cheddar.

Finely chop, then stir-fry in sesame oil with lightly toasted peanuts. Serve with noodles and chilli sauce.

Make a new version of 'tortilla'. Finely chop the vegetables, mix with seasoning and enough beaten eggs to cover. Heat a frying-pan and, when hot, add a generous amount of olive oil. Pour in the mixture and stir gently for 1 minute. Cook until set.

Shred your left-over salad greens. Heat some olive oil in a pan, add a handful of pinenuts and cook until golden, then add the greens, some ground black pepper and salt. Toss with tagliatelle or spaghetti and freshly squeezed lemon juice, then smother with freshly grated parmesan.

THE STORE CUPBOARD
FRIDGE & PANTRY

When I was growing up in Wanganui, New Zealand, I dreamed of having a store-cupboard or walk-in pantry. It seemed as though every television family had one, but all we had was a set of cupboards above the kitchen worktops. . . And here I am at thirty-six and all I have are those cupboards above the worktops! Which is all I really need because now I have a big fridge too. The cupboards and worktops are crammed with spices, vinegars, grains, oils and provisions, so now I dream of a big cellar for my preserves and chutneys, where it's always cool and dark . . . but that will have to be in another house.

I keep most of my home-made pickles, relishes and chutneys in the fridge, which takes up a lot of the space.

Sometimes it seems too huge an effort to get out the preserving pan and set in motion the whole sterilising process. I promise myself, though, that when I finally get my cellar, I'll be bottling like there's no tomorrow. I'm looking forward to turning on the cellar light and seeing gleaming jars of pickled figs, syrup-drenched peaches and tomato chutney.

All the following relishes, chutneys and jams can be stored out of the fridge if you are familiar with preserving and the techniques to keep food safely for periods of time. For these recipes, though, I have suggested they be stored in the fridge so that they will keep with no risk to you. It is essential that all jars are cleaned thoroughly before use: I add 100 g of salt to every litre of boiling water and pour this into the jars, leaving them for 5 minutes before rinsing them with boiled water. Soak the lids in this brine as well.

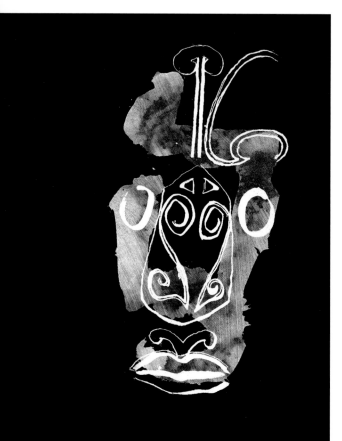

tomato sauce for pasta

The best time to make this is just before the end of summer, when tomatoes are at their cheapest, sweetest and best. To preserve it, you'll have to get out the waxy seals or the bottling kit, but it will keep for up to a week in the fridge, if properly sealed. This rich, oily sauce is my own personal favourite, tossed through spaghettini with some wilted watercress and parmesan for a quick supper, layered between lasagne with left-over roast lamb and béchamel sauce for brunch, or smothered over salmon and baked on top of pre-cooked penne for dinner. I add carrot, beetroot and red peppers for a bit of body, and you may need to put in a touch of sugar and lemon juice at the end of cooking if your tomatoes aren't the best.

FOR 2.5 LITRES, ENOUGH FOR 15-20 PASTA PORTIONS

large red onions	*3, peeled and sliced*
garlic	*8 cloves, peeled and roughly chopped*
hot red chilli	*1, sliced*
red peppers	*2, seeds and stem removed, roughly chopped*
fresh rosemary	*1 tablespoon, chopped*
extra-virgin olive oil	*200 ml*
dried oregano	*2 teaspoons*
bay leaves	*2*
medium carrot	*1, peeled and coarsely grated*
medium cooked beetroot	*1, peeled and coarsely grated*
tomatoes	*1.5 kg, roughly chopped*
cider vinegar	*50 ml*
fresh basil leaves	*2 large handfuls*
salt	
black pepper	*freshly ground*

Put the first 5 ingredients with the oil into a large saucepan and cook over a moderately high heat, stirring occasionally, until the onions begin to brown. Add all the remaining ingredients except the basil, bring to the boil, then turn to a rapid simmer and cook for 15–25 minutes, until the sauce just begins to thicken as the liquid evaporates. Leave it to cool to the point where you can handle it without burning yourself, remove the bay leaves, and roughly blend it in either a food-processor or liquidiser. Then tear the basil leaves roughly by hand and stir them into the sauce. Taste for seasoning. Either use it straight away, or leave it to cool completely before you store it in the fridge in sealed jars.

sozzled cherries

These days, cherries are around for months in the summer and at odd times of the year, but I make this when they are in season and try to keep some for next year – then they're really great. Serve with anything from ice cream to steamed winter puddings, and have the liquor as a night-cap whenever it seems like a good idea. Make sure, though, that if you're taking out more liquor than cherries you keep them covered by topping up with alcohol.

It's best that the jar is fully loaded with fruit, and the best way to make sure that your jar is the right size is to fill it with fresh cherries, then tip them out and weigh them. Base the weights and volumes that you'll need on this measurement. Make sure the alcohol completely fills the jar, and that your seal is airtight.

FOR 1 KG CHERRIES AND 750 ML LIQUOR

caster sugar	*400 g*
runny honey	*100 ml, preferably orange-blossom*
water	*100 ml*
clove	*1*
orange	*juice and peel (no pith) of 1*
cherries	*1 kg, washed, drained, stems removed, pricked twice with a needle*
cointreau	*300 ml*
white rum	*300 ml*

Put the sugar, honey, water, clove, orange juice and peel into a saucepan, stir well and bring to the boil. Boil for 3 minutes then leave to cool. Warm a preserving jar just large enough to hold all the cherries, place them in it and pour over the cooled syrup. Pour on enough alcohol to cover the fruit – you may need more or less than the quantities given above, then seal the jar. Turn it upside down every day for 2 weeks, and leave for at least 2 months in a cool dark place before using.

dried fruit and walnut chutney

This is best made at least a week and preferably a month in advance of when you want to eat it. As it uses dried fruit, it isn't particularly seasonal, but it goes really well with anything from cured meats to blue cheeses, roast lamb, the Christmas ham or grilled field mushrooms on toast.

FOR APPROXIMATELY 1 LITRE

olive oil	*60 ml*
walnut pieces	*200 g, or walnut halves, roughly chopped*
fresh rosemary	*1 teaspoon, finely chopped*
sultanas	*200 g*
raisins	*100 g*
demerara sugar	*100 g (or use coconut sugar)*
cider vinegar	*400 ml*
crystallised ginger	*100 g, finely sliced*
dried apricots	*300 g, cut in half*
pitted prunes	*100 g, roughly chopped*
sea salt	*1/2 teaspoon*
nutmeg	*1/2 teaspoon, freshly grated*
ground allspice	*2 teaspoons*

Heat a large saucepan on the stove and put in the oil, then fry the nuts until they are golden. Add the rosemary, sultanas, raisins and sugar and fry them until the fruit begins to caramelise. Pour in the vinegar and boil on a high heat for 3 minutes. Then add the rest of the ingredients, bring to the boil, then turn to a simmer and cook until most of the liquid has evaporated. Because of the dried fruit, this chutney has a tendency to stick to the bottom of the pan, so stir it well and keep an eye on it. Spoon it into clean hot jars, filling them as full as you can, and seal while still hot. Store in the fridge.

roast nectarine and red onion chutney

This oven-cooked chutney can be made using any stone fruit, but I made it first with nectarines so my loyalty lies with them. Serve it with grilled pork, roast chicken or on grilled sourdough bread with goat's cheese and raw spinach. As with most chutneys and relishes, the flavours develop after a week so leave it if you can. In the recipe you'll notice I use a *farcellet*, which is a dried bouquet garni from Barcelona. You will be fine if you substitute it with dried bay leaves, though.

FOR APPROXIMATELY 2 KG

nectarines	*15, stoned and quartered*
garlic	*4 cloves, peeled and roughly chopped*
medium red onions	*8, peeled and finely sliced*
lemon	*1, halved then finely sliced, pips removed*
fresh rosemary leaves	*2 tablespoons*
farcellet	*1 or a few dried bay leaves*
cumin seeds	*1 teaspoon*
fennel seeds	*1 teaspoon*
cider vinegar	*250 ml*
demerara sugar	*400 g*
thai fish sauce	*3 teaspoons*

Pre-heat the oven to 200°c.

Put everything except the sugar and fish sauce into a large non-reactive ovenproof dish and mix well. Place in the upper half of the oven and cook for 1 hour, stirring from time to time. Once the chutney begins to bubble and caramelise, add the sugar and the fish sauce and cook for a further 30-40 minutes, stirring twice during this time. The chutney should be a little moist and the fruit still discernible in shape. If it is still too wet, continue to cook. Spoon the chutney into warmed preserving jars, seal while hot and let it cool before storing in the fridge. Leave for at least a week before eating.

vanilla sugar

vanilla pods	*4*
caster sugar	*1 kg*

My version of vanilla sugar is rough but very tasty and looks good in a jar. You can make it with either regular or unrefined sugar. It will keep for up to 8 months.

Cut the vanilla pods into 8 pieces each. Place them in a food-processor, then add half of the sugar. Blitz for 1 minute, then scrape the sides of the bowl and process again for 2 minutes. Mix with the remaining sugar, transfer into a clean jar and store out of direct light.

When you want to use it, stir it well – it sometimes forms lumps – then pour the required amount of sugar through a sieve. Return the bits to the jar, add a little more sugar, stir well and reseal.

spicy preserved figs

I like to make these in late autumn when the last of the figs are around, with the intention of eating them in the new year with air-dried English ham, or a *jamòn* from Spain. Usually, when you cut one open, you find a generous amount of natural jelly inside from the pectin in the pips. If your figs are large, and you find you don't have enough liquid to cover them from the quantities given below, just boil up some more and pour it over them. I like to use purple figs for this, but green ones work just as well.

FOR A 1 X 2.5 LITRE JAR

cider vinegar	*400 ml, or white wine vinegar*
water	*800 ml*
cinnamon stick	*1, broken up*
cloves	*3*
cardamom pods	*4, crushed*
hot red chilli	*1, sliced*
fresh ginger	*2 thumbs, peeled and roughly chopped*
garlic	*2 cloves, peeled and roughly chopped*
unrefined caster sugar	*450 g*
sea salt	*2 teaspoons*
ripe figs	*12-15*

Place everything except the figs in a saucepan and boil gently, uncovered, for 5 minutes. Meanwhile, rinse out a 2.5-litre heatproof bottling jar with hot water, then drain and dry, and put in the figs. Pack them in tightly but be careful not to break the skins. Warm the jar by sitting it in a saucepan with enough hot water to come a third of the way up it. Once the liquid is ready, pour it over the figs, getting in as much of the spices as possible and making sure that the figs are covered with the pickling liquid. Close the jar and seal it, then leave it to cool. Once it is cold, place in the fridge upside-down for a day, then turn it right side up and leave it for between 3 weeks and 3 months before using.

roasted peanut and cashew butter

I remember thinking as a child that peanut butter must be hard to make. How, for example, did they mix the butter into the peanuts? One day I saw American peanut butter and jelly in a jar, in strange brown and red stripes. It was too much to think about. In my late teens, I saw an even stranger sight: a peanut-butter machine. All you'll need for this, though, is an oven and a food-processor.

MAKES APPROXIMATELY 500 G

unsalted roasted peanuts	*300 g*
toasted cashew nuts	*200 g*
salt to taste	
peanut or salad oil	*optional*

Put everything in a food-processor and grind at full speed until you have a paste, scraping down the sides as you go. This can take up to 8 minutes. If you find that you just end up with finely ground nuts, add up to 50 ml peanut (or salad) oil to help it along. If you want 'crunchy' rather than 'smooth' peanut butter, save 200 g of the nuts until the paste has formed, then add them at the end and grind to your desired texture.

Keep this in a cool place at all times of year, but definitely in the fridge during the summer.

garlic butter

Another thing I bought from one of the Orford smokehouses was some smoked garlic. With it I made the most delicious smoked-garlic butter, which reinvented mushrooms on toast the next morning. (Of course, you can use regular garlic instead.) Use it in garlic bread, that old bistro favourite, which I love, or fry onions and veggies for soup in it, brush it on chops and fish at the last minute of grilling, or spread it in cheese sandwiches and grill them.

salted butter	*250 g, at room temperature*
extra-virgin olive oil	*50 ml*
garlic	*8 cloves, peeled and finely chopped*
a bunch of chives	*finely sliced*

Either whisk the butter and oil together by hand until fluffy, or whiz them in a food-processor. Mix in the garlic and chives, and a few grindings of black pepper. Store in the fridge for up to 2 weeks.

anchovy butter

Anchovy butter is a lovely rich 'taste-adder' to have on hand. It keeps in the fridge for a week, so if the quantities seem more than you think you could use in a meal for two, don't worry. Try it melted into pasta with broccoli, dolloped on to grilled fish or barbecued lamb chops; spread it instead of regular butter in a chicken sandwich, or have it on toast with really sweet tomatoes and chives.

Ideally, you would make it from salted anchovies that you have scaled, rinsed and boned, but you can use good anchovies preserved in oil: you might need to add a few extra of the latter as they don't taste as strong.

salted anchovy fillets *10*
unsalted butter *250 g, at room temperature*
spring onions *2, finely sliced*
olive oil *80 ml*

Place everything in a food-processor and purée to a paste, scraping down the bowl as you go. It should take about 30 seconds. Alternatively, you could finely chop the anchovies and beat them into the butter with the spring onions. Place it in a jar and store in the fridge for up to a week. Always use it at room temperature, at which point it will melt lovingly over whatever you choose.

olive oil butter

I like this butter because it's easier to spread straight from the fridge on breakfast toast, and I love the taste of olive oil. Not that I'd recommend you use it with strawberry jam. I always make it with unsalted butter, in case I want to eat it with bacon or other salty meats or fish.

unsalted butter *250 g, at room temperature*
extra-virgin olive oil *120 ml*

Either whisk the butter and oil together by hand, or whiz them in a food-processor, until light and fluffy. Store in the fridge for up to 2 weeks.

spiced nuts

These nuts will keep in an airtight jar in a dark place for up to 1 month. They're handy to have in the cupboard for snacks at parties, for when you have the munchies, and they've helped sustain me while I was writing this book and when I needed a bit of palate stimulation. Take my basic principle here and use whatever spices you want. The reason I cook them in separate batches is that nuts cook at differing speeds, depending on their size, oil content, etc. However, you could cook them all at once in the same oven on separate trays.

MAKES 500 G, ENOUGH FOR COCKTAIL NIBBLES FOR 10 OR MORE

icing sugar	*80 g*
sweet smoked paprika	*1 level dessertspoon*
cumin seeds	*2 teaspoons*
fennel seeds	*2 teaspoons*
kalonji (black onion) seeds	*2 teaspoons*
fresh rosemary	*1 teaspoon, finely chopped*
sesame seeds	*3 teaspoons*
extra-virgin olive oil	*50 ml*
sea salt	*11/2 teaspoons*
brazil nuts	*100 g*
cashew nuts	*100 g*
almonds	*100 g*
pecan nuts	*100 g*
pinenuts	*100 g*

Pre-heat the oven to 180°c. Mix together the first 9 ingredients into a paste, then divide it among 5 bowls, then add 1 batch of nuts to each bowl and mix well with the paste. Lay the nuts on baking-parchment-lined baking-trays and cook them until each batch is deeply golden and aromatic. The pinenuts should cook quickest, in about 10-15 minutes, then a race will be on for the rest. Leave them to cool on their trays before mixing them together and storing in an airtight jar.

green herb oil

More and more often when you go to a restaurant you'll find a lovely green oil, fragrant with herbs, drizzled over your grilled swordfish, goat's cheese salad or poached chicken breast. Flavoured oils are easy to make, and add a lovely finish to a simple dish. They taste truly delicious too. My favourite herbs to use are basil, mint, tarragon and oregano, but a combination of several can be truly inspiring. Keep the oil in a cool, dark place, and it will stay fragrant for a month.

FOR 500 ML

herb of your choice	*1 large coffee mug, tightly packed with leaves*
light-tasting oil	*300 ml, for example, sunflower, light olive oil*
extra-virgin olive oil	*200 ml*

Bring a litre of water to the boil then plunge in the herbs and stir gently. Leave them for 2 seconds, then strain them through a sieve. Tip the herbs into a bowl of iced water and leave them to chill for a minute, gently stirring once. Remove them and drain well, then pat them dry with a tea-towel or absorbent paper. Place them in a liquidiser with the light oil, and blend for 30 seconds. Leave it to sit for 10 minutes, then strain through a fine sieve into a clean jar or bottle. (You can either discard the sediment or brush it on fish when it's almost cooked.) Stir in the extra-virgin olive oil and it's ready to drizzle.

index

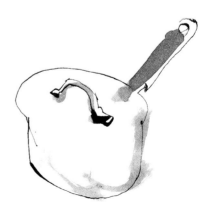